A DANCE OF LIGHT AND DARK

—

Poetry from the Heart

A DANCE of LIGHT and DARK

Poetry from the Heart

Anne Pollard and Jerry L. Style

A Dance of Light and Dark - Poetry from the Heart

Printed in the United States of America
ISBN 978-1-967279-20-3 (hc)
ISBN 978-1-967279-21-0 (sc)
ISBN 978-1-967279-22-7 (e)

2025.03.04

This book is printed on acid-free paper.

The contents of this work, including, but not limited to, the accuracy of events, people, and places depicted; opinions expressed; permission to use previously published materials included; and any advice given or actions advocated are solely the responsibility of the author, who assumes all liability for said work and indemnifies the publisher against any claims stemming from publication of the work.

Blue Ink Media Solutions
1111B S Governors Ave
STE 7582 Dover,
DE 19904
www.blueinkmediasolutions.com

Table of Contents

A Dance of Light and Dark

They met through a club
   And became instant friends
   Both of them poets at heart
But they didn't predict
   That a book would be born –
   Dancing between light and dark

Their muses were different
   Both born to a life of
   Different paths to be sure
Weaving the tales
   That shaped both their lives –
   Poetry was always the cure

When life knocks you down
   Do you look for the joy?
   Or instead – scream out in pain?
Do you look past the hurt
   And forever hope
   That it will never happen again?

Is cold simply the absence of heat?
   Is darkness, absence of light?
   Or are the opposites true?
Is how you deal
   With life's ups and downs
   Depend on your point of view?

So come with us now
   On a journey of life
   Whether joyous or equally stark,
As you move through
   all the many emotions
   In a Dance of Light and Dark

by Anne Pollard
and Jerry Style

Dedication

Dedicated to all those who struggle with life's ups and downs, to those who find joy in everyday living, and for everyone in between.

To those celebrating or searching for answers from different points of view.

BEFORE THE DAWN

BEFORE NIGHT BECOMES TOMORROW,

WHEN MIST HINTS OF A BREAKING DAY,

WHEN THE MOON BEGINS TO FADE IN SORROW

KNOWING THE SUN WILL STEAL ITS NIGHT AWAY.

WHEN SILENCE AND DARKNESS MAKE PERFECT COVERS

FOR TWO HEARTS CRAVING WARM EMBRACES,

WHEN IN THE SHADOWS, THOSE TANGLED LOVERS,

FORCE LONELINESS TO RETREAT WITHOUT ANY TRACES.

WHEN REFLECTING ON THIS SPECIAL TIME

WHEN OUR HEARTS AND YEARNING SOULS DID UNITE,

KNOW THAT THIS PREDAWN UNION SUBLIME,

BROUGHT US OUT OF DARKNESS AND INTO THE LIGHT

By Jerry L Style

Today, I Choose Joy

I woke this morning a little groggy
Autumn mist, and kinda foggy
No sunshine to deploy
But today, I choose joy

The news was full of war again
When does hatred finally end
And men who seek to destroy
But today, I choose joy

It's not that I don't feel for those
Who struggle through the daily throws
I don't use it as an emotional decoy
But today, I choose joy

And when you hold it in your heart
A new earth consciousness will start
And this we can all employ
So today, I choose joy

It holds the highest frequency
And spreads like fire for all to see
Creates the world we most enjoy
So today, I choose joy

It's a choice you make every day
What emotions come and stay
And like a child with a brand-new toy
Today, I Choose Joy

By Anne Pollard

BEAUTY

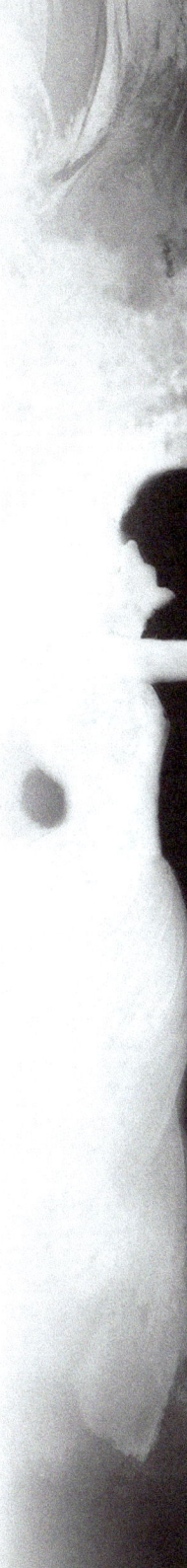

"Old man," he cried, "I've come so far.
I'm so tired, I can go no more.
But that I seek, seems all but lost.
Can't find what I've been looking for."

"My life's so empty, my heart so sick.
I feel such anguish, hurting, fear.
For pain and hatred, sadness and greed,
Is all I see and all I hear."

"It's beauty I need, and love and peace,
Pleasure, happiness, caring, grace.
I know it's out there! Help me please!
Help me find that beautiful place!"

The old man sighed; his face went dim.
In life, he was watching the setting sun.
After a pause, he took a deep breath.
"You are now ready to see beauty, my son."

But he said no more, his eyes were closed.
Anger welled up in the young man's soul.
"Tell me how!" he cried, "Don't die now!
You have the answer I need to know!"

As he sat and watched his setting sun,
The old man's eyes opened, full of tears.
He'd been there before; he knew of the pain.
He felt the man's anguish, knew of his fears.

His face was scarred with life's toil and pain,
Showing the years of his suffering past.
But now in his eyes was a look of true peace,
And after seeming eternity, he spoke at last.

3

"You are lucky my son to feel as you do.
For you can now see what the others all miss.
There's a purpose for suffering, a reason for pain.
The answer my son is simply this."

"To feel pleasure, one must first feel pain.
To know peace, despair; pride, shame;
To feel caring, distain; and charity, greed;
Happiness, sadness; praise, blame."

"You have felt the things bad, now all that remains
Is to find from those terrible things – the good.
You'll find it in places you'd never look.
And look in those places you never would."

"Don't look for beauty in a pretty face.
It's much deeper than that, but here's a clue.
Beauty is in someone who shows life's scars.
You'll find beauty in someone who finds beauty in you."

By Jerry L Style

The Full Blue Moon

as i sat quietly to go within
to seek the source of pain
electrical currents flow through my skin
as if a pouring rain

the addiction was calling loud and fast
it sought to take control
was it a vision from the past
or a trauma yet to unfold

unable to quelch the maddening need
i gave into it again
it comes with such a force and speed
but where did it begin

i asked my intuition to help me see the light
but i am answered with only black
i push and force with all my might
but the demon just comes back

does the answer lie in the full blue moon
can i find the key
the promise of new beginnings soon
will ultimately set me free

for the answer lies within, i know
my guide the morning dove
stop the force and let it flow
and choose to live in love

By Anne Pollard

My Father's Eyes

"Does anyone wish to say anything?"
the undertaker said.
But I sat there in silence and said not a thing,
Not believing my father was dead.
He had suffered, you see, but the pain was away
As I filed in to say my goodbyes.
But the man that I saw in the coffin that day
Did not have my father's eyes.

For with his eyes closed, they show no emotion,
I could not look into his heart.
And without his eyes, there was no communication,
No real way for us to depart.
And I thought as I sat there of things that were,
Of things that most logic denies,
That my life with my father was like a mirror
Reflected in my father's eyes.

For when I played him a song, or hit a home run,
The pride was so easy to see.
Or when he told a tall tale or a little pun,
His eyes were all filled with glee.
And when I hurt him so bad, all too often my goal;
A fact that my heart now decries,
I could see the pain go down to his soul;
Deep in my father's eyes.

And when dad finally entered his waning years,
His lips seldom uttered a word.
But his eyes were alive with his pain, love and fears,
Though the words seldom ever were heard.
And when coma took over and everyone bet
That he's met his final demise,
It was just that his heart didn't know it yet,
But there was death in my father's eyes.

A Dance of Light and Dark

You see, it wasn't with words that dad showed his emotion;
Not the way others usually do.
It was with his eyes that he showed his pride and devotion;
With his eyes he said, "I love you!"
Not many spoke in this language of sight
And I wondered if I was that wise.
Did my love for him show? Did it shine real bright?
Was it seen by my father's eyes?

"Does anyone wish to say anything?"
the undertaker repeated.
But we sat there in silence and said not a thing.
The spoken word had been defeated.
But we were all there, and loved one another.
It could not be otherwise.
As we sat there in silence, consoling each other
Using the words of my father's eyes.

By Jerry L Style

Hiawatha

He came in a vision
This warrior man
     Tall and proud
     Mystic wisdom
Guiding my plan

He stood beside
A lifeless deer
     Rose from death
     Bringing peace
But without tear

Hiawatha, he said
Calling his name
     Indian strong
     Great Spirit
One and the same

We spoke for hours
Big things will bloom
     Transformation
     Enlightenment
Before the next full moon

Let me guide you
Stay in the flow
     Release
     Control
Let it all go

Things will unfold
Steps each day
     Patience
     Trust
The Indian way

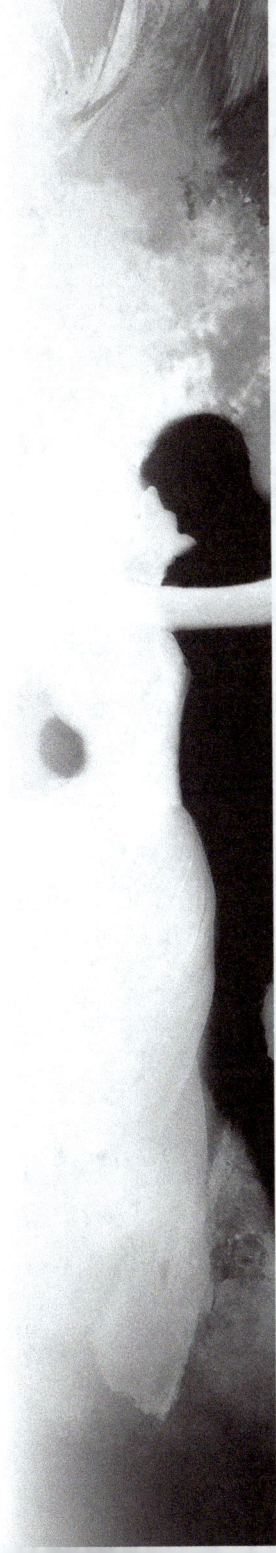

A Dance of Light and Dark

Your path is assured
Your heart is pure
     Like the deer
     Back to spirit
Oneness is yours

My journey is short
Time's blink of an eye
     Great life circle
     As deer disappears
So will I

By Anne Pollard

Where does God live?

The March night sky was moonless and clear
But thousands of stars shared their light,
And the frost all around made the world appear
Draped in shimmering diamonds of the night.
Though winter had battered those who live here
With a torrent of fury and might
It was apparent that life would soon persevere;
Winter's death-grip was losing the fight.

But winter was not yet ready to quit;
Not ready to give up on death,
As an old man and young boy watched the skies starlit,
Clouds of frost formed with every breath.
Content to stay beneath stars they were under;
There's no hurry to flee the night air.
They gazed at the sky with awe and wonder
And the grandfather whispered a prayer.

He prayed that God watch over his wife
Who he's lost oh, so long ago.
And he thanked God for bringing to his lonely life
This little grandson that he loved so.
And he asked for the patience in raising the lad
And the courage, understanding and might
To keep from the child influences that were bad
And the wisdom to know wrong from right.

Then he begged God to forgive his wayward son
Who had abandoned his wife and this child.
Then he tried to explain to the Holy One
Though his son had been reckless and wild
That the young man was really quite good at heart
And that he, the father, was to blame;
That he hadn't spent time with his son from the start,
And for that he felt guilt and shame.

The little one watched on patiently
As the old man asked God to forgive.
"Amen." Then the small one asked innocently,
"Gramps, where does God live?"
The old man admired the child's need to know,
And he smiled at the youth with love.
Then he pointed up to the skies starry show.
"He's with Grandma in Heaven above."

The little guy stopped and thought for a bit,
A puzzled look on his face.
"But Grandpa," he said, "that can't be it!
The astronauts been up there in space.
And I know that they looked everywhere!
They'd a seen Heaven, Gramps, wouldn't ya say?
And besides, it's way far away up there!
God couldn't hear us when we pray!"

Surprised by the questions of his little grandson,
The old man recalled times when he'd say
To his own boy, "Sorry, I've got things to get done,
We'll talk about it later, OK?"
But later never came, so this time he'd try
To help the young tyke in his search.
"You might be right," he said with a sigh.
"Well, some say that God lives in church."

Not happy with that, the boy wouldn't give in.
"I've thought about that, Gramps, before.
But there are so many churches, which one does God live in?
And then, what are all the other churches for?"
The old man was stunned, stood there dumbfounded
Why different religions? Youth with questions so old!
And questions for eons that left scholars confounded.
He started to sweat spite the cold.

Much to Grandpa's relief, before he replied,
The young lad pressed on in his search.
"And if Grandma's with God, n' everyone else who died,
There wouldn't be 'nough room in the church!
And where would God eat, take a bath, watch TV?
And I never seen a bed there, have you?"
Then with a glint in his eye, he quipped playfully,
"Does God sleep during church like you do?"

The unlikely pair roared in laughter together,
And Grampa cried, "Now hold on there, Smarty-Pants!
You ask all your questions one after another
So you never give me a chance!
Since you don't like any answer I said,
You tell me since you think you're so smart!"
The little one suddenly went quiet, hung his head.
"Mom says God lives in your heart."

The old man knelt down to the level of the boy,
Then the tyke hugged his Grandpa so tight
That the show of affection filled the old man with joy.
He whispered, "You know, I think your mommy's right."
The lad then unbuttoned his grandfather's coat
And pressed his ear so tightly to his chest.
He stayed there a while, then with a quirk in his throat
"Grandpa, I think you're the best!"

"An', if God is livin' in a heart somewhere,
I know that he must be in you!
But I listened, and he doesn't seem to be there.
Maybe he's asleep, but I still think it's true."
The old man then put his ear near the heart of the lad.
"Wait, wait! I hear something!" he cried.
"It's saying, 'Me want cooky an' milk real bad!'
Let's go get some from mommy inside!"

A Dance of Light and Dark

The giggling duet entered the house, faces red.
Mom asked, "And what have you boys been up to?"
"Just talking," the boy laughed. "Man stuff," Grampa said.
Mom replied, "I'm starting to worry about you two.
I just made some cookies. Want some? I'm a good cook!"
The two looked at each other and exploded.
They snickered with every bit of cookie they took,
Their funny bones overloaded.

Then Grandpa collected some logs and started a fire,
And Mom took the tyke in to get clean.
Then the small one scurried down in his nighttime attire,
His freckled face neatly scrubbed to a sheen.
He ran to his Grandpa and took a flying leap
Onto the old man's lap, wanting to play games.
But instead they snuggled together, ready for sleep
As they sat there watching the flames.

The room was all dark but for the light given off
By the fire in the hearth burning bright,
And all in the room were covered in a soft
Bath of orangy, flickering light.
The old man and boy watch the fire entranced
As waves of heat wash over them as they lay.
And the shadows created all around them danced
Like scores of frisky kittens at play.

The small one was pensive and let out a long sigh.
Gently he started to sway.
And while fighting all his temptations to cry
Said, "Grandpa, why did my Daddy run away?"
The old man had feared that question for years,
Never knowing just what he would say.
While he took out a tissue to dry the boy's tears
Whispered, "Well, maybe we'll understand that someday."

"But you're so nice, Grandpa, and Mommy is, too!
Did he run 'cause he didn't like me?"
"No way!" Grandpa scolded, "it wasn't because of you!
Your daddy's just a little mixed up, you see.
He really is good" he said going out on a limb,
Making promise for the absentee.
"He's just forgotten what's important to him,
Like his home and his family."

The old man felt the guilt bearing down on his soul
And to the boy was about to confess
Of his neglect as a father and his loss of control,
But was asked "Does that mean that my Daddy is homeless?"
"I guess you might say that," the old man replied,
"And I don't know about you or your Mom,
But if your Dad comes home sorry, and puts his bad ways aside,
He'll be able to call <u>this</u> place his home."

"I'll never run away, Gramps! I Promise!" the boy said
As he snuggled in to get close.
Then he noticed the warmth and love the house shed.
"And besides, I like bein' in your house!"
"And I promise you this," the old man vowed,
"That as long as you or your Mom desire
That this will be <u>your</u> home and that I will be proud
To do whatever our lives may require!"

For the first time in his life, the boy felt he belonged,
And he loved feeling safe and secure.
Though such a young age, he'd been rejected and wronged,
So he knew what it took to endure.
He felt washed with unconditional love and acceptance
But instinctively thought of those with much less,
Of those who had never gotten this loving chance,
So he asked, "Grandpa, why are some people homeless?"

"Boy, you ask tough questions!" the old man said
As he rubbed his unshaven gray chin.
"Different reasons, I guess, some want that instead,
But most are too poor, or just don't fit in.
But the real problem is that not enough people care
To help the homeless get their lives looking up,
But somehow, I think you'll make a difference out there,
That is, of course, when you're done growing up."

"But I don't wanna wait till I get big!" the boy cried,
"I wanna do som'pin' 'bout it right now!"
"Well, the most you can do right now," Grandpa replied
"Is to show people that they should care somehow."
"Well, I'm gonna do som'pin', I really will Gramps!"
"I'm sure you will, my Little Crusader!"
And the weary two sat there, battered world saving champs
Fighting a cunning and ruthless invader.

"It's getting late, Little Guy, best get to bed.
Sounds like you'll have a busy day tomorrow."
"But Grandpa, please can I stay with you instead?"
So, he gave the little one more time to borrow.
But in minutes he fell asleep in his grandfather's arms,
Content with loves generous reward,
Feeling protected from life's many pitfalls and harms,
The little one quietly snored.

The old man rubbed the hair of the boy, fast asleep,
Impressed with the little one's trust.
And he searched through his memory ever so deep
To find other times when his presence was a must.
He's been needed in the past, but for money and support,
But he couldn't recall need for his love like this before.
And if his love had been needed, his time was cut short
By the overwhelming material needs that life bore.

15

He carried the little cherub, asleep, off to bed,
　　　Tucked him in and gave him a kiss.
　　Then he returned to the fire and rested his head.
　　　He listened to its burning, muffled hiss.
Its life was dying out now. Mostly embers there glowed,
　　But a random burst of flame would rise and fall.
And as his eyes looked 'round the room, they soon took a hold
On his wife's picture looking down on him from the wall.

　　The old man looked away, afraid to look her in the eye.
　　　The guilt he felt brought him such shame
　　That 'til now he couldn't face her; he had wanted to die.
　　But an inner strength rose in him and he called her name.
　　　"I miss you so much," he sobbed tearfully,
　　"And I'm sorry I haven't spoken to you since you died.
　　　But I've been living my life so regretfully
　　　That, to be honest, I haven't even tried."

　　　"I've thought about my life so much of late,
　　And _you_ know that in life, I couldn't have tried harder.
　　　But no matter my moves, I'd be in checkmate,
　　　I've been feeling that I was life's martyr.
　　　When we needed a break, we never got one.
　　When things looked good, something changed them to bad.
　　　When God handed out blessings, we seemed forgotten.
　　　We broke our back for all that we had."

　　　"Remember when we were first married
　　And you became pregnant almost right away?
　　　We were flying so high that it carried
　　　Us to tremendous heights, 'til that awful day.
　　　That one day changed our lives forever
　　　When you lost the baby and we cried.
　　So we hoped and we hoped for another and another,
　　　But couldn't, though hundreds of doctors tried."

16

"Years and years went by, then we found you were sick,
And just when all hope seemed gone away
We were called by the agency and told to pick
Up our new son at the hospital right away.
I'll never forget the look on your face
When I told you the wonderful news.
We ran around like maniacs, all over the place.
So excited, we forgot to wear shoes!"

"That night, at home, was the best night of my life.
I've never felt such complete contentment.
Lying in bed with my four-day old son and my wife.
But you guessed it! The next day brought resentment!
The lawyer called us with his message of pain.
Said that the mother wanted the baby back.
But then she changed her mind, again and again.
It's a wonder we didn't have a heart attack!"

"For years we lived in fear of a telephone's ring,
But the years passed in spite of our fright.
But through those years, we began to notice something.
Something about our son was not quite right.
We didn't know what it really was at first,
But we prayed about it nightly to the Above.
Then the doctors gave us the word, the worst!
Our son was partly autistic and incapable of love."

"Throughout all of this, I worked day and night,
Trying to pay every bill.
All the doctors, all the lawyers, all a parasite!
All trying to break our will.
And they succeeded, you know, they all did the trick
In taking what little in life that we had.
Because you just thought of me as a workaholic,
And our son never did have a dad."

"Then came that fateful night, our boy was sixteen,
When I just couldn't take anymore!
I went out that night and I drank and got mean,
Then came home like a wild raging boar.
And I fought with our son, and I drove him away,
And I'll know 'til my dying breath
That the battle that I had with our son that day
Broke your heart, and years later caused your death."

"And the pain, in my heart, of that day, still lives on!
Kept alive in my blackened soul.
But it's also in his wife, and our little grandson,
Pulling in like a massive black hole!
What was it in life that caused all this pain?
What caused me so much to loathe?
Was it God forsaking me? Or my failures again and again?
I've gone through life hating me and Him both!"

"But I've been doing the things you told me to do.
Probably things you'd never conceive.
I've been going to church, and praying, too.
But to be honest, I still don't believe.
But I felt something stir in my heart today, Hon.
It took me completely by surprise.
It came from the heart of our little grandson.
He's so young, but so incredibly wise.

"You'd love him, Sweetheart. I wish that you'd met.
He brings a smile to this bitter man's face.
Do you think that there's really some hope for me yet?
Is God really living someplace?"
The old man's eyes from the picture fell.
He laughed that he could again feel joy.
Then there on the couch, into a deep sleep he fell,
And he dreamt of the little boy.

18

A Dance of Light and Dark

The fire had raged on in its valiant warfare
Striving to keep the room bathed in its light.
But, alas, this violent marriage of wood and air
Was doomed from ever winning the fight.
The room was in silence but for the old man's breathing,
Or a pop of an occasional spark.
And the smoke drifted upward, as if it were grieving
The impending blackness of the dark.

Into the darkness the boy's mom entered the room.
She made sure that the fire was out.
Then she spied the old man who sleep did consume,
And she tried to alleviate her doubt.
Did she do the right thing by moving in here?
Though it wasn't like she ever had a choice.
But she could still hear her husband say, crystal clear,
"Stay away from my old man!" in his hateful voice.

But she had moved all around from one place to another
With her little baby boy in tow.
And she struggled to be both a bread-winner and mother,
But it just wasn't working, she'd know.
So when the old man offered that they live in his place,
At first, she quickly declined.
But how could she, when the cost of a sitter would outpace
The money she made, and leave her in a bind?

Yet the old man seemed so angry, almost rabid.
How would he be with her little son?
Would her baby grow up the way her husband did?
God, what an impossible situation!
Eventually she decided to move into his home,
Having no choice, forced to give it a try.
But she also decided that she would continue to comb
Other options with time now to buy.

Yet, something happened today, something profound,
To her, just what it was, was unknown.
But for a while it felt as if she had found
A place they could comfortably call home.
And her little one seemed to find something here,
Something he really did miss.
So she stood there and smiled down on the old volunteer
Bent over and gently gave him a kiss.

She, too, went to bed holding a feeling of hope,
Though there was no one else there to hold.
She began to feel safe and able to cope
With her world which had been brutal and hard.
She thought of her husband, though she tried to be loving,
It never did seem quite enough.
She was surprised that she no longer felt the guilt in his leaving
And in the darkness, she softly dozed off.

The dark pre-dawn sky was still eager to bemuse
Those below, pushing all to the brink.
But it was losing control, and like a healing bruise
Changed from black to a gray shade of pink.
And the stars began fading, losing their luster,
Giving up their futile try to light the way.
Though the night fought on with all the strength it could muster
It knew that soon it would surrender to the day.

One by one, the sun's rays began breaking through,
And like the crack in the proverbial dam,
Each one was followed by another two
Until a deluge of light 'round earth swam.
Morning had broken in a glorious display
Of the sun's awesome power and might.
And the light it shed welcomed a brand-new day
And bid adieu to the pain of the night.

A Dance of Light and Dark

As the rays came down, they danced all around
    And all the signs of the night withdrew.
And the sunshine heated all things on the ground,
    Converting frost to a sparkling dew.
A few lucky rays were awarded the prize
    Of shining down on the little boy's bed.
They caressed the boy's face and tickled his eyes
    Saying, "Wake up, Little Sleepy-Head!"

The little boy stirred and at first was annoyed
    By the light invading his cozy warm bed.
And bothersome thoughts in the small one toyed
    Like a pesky fly buzzing 'round his head.
He had hated the mornings, 'cause what it meant
Was that mom would go to work, leaving him there
    With all sorts of strange people who only spent
    Their time watching TV or combing their hair.

But when he opened his eyes and remembered he was where
    Things were different, he lost his regret.
So, he jumped out of bed and bound down the stair,
    Clamoring down like a marionette.
He burst into the kitchen with such a loud shout
That it caught his mom and Grandpa by surprise.
They ate breakfast together, Mom rose to go out,
    Kissed her son and they said their goodbyes.

As Mom walked out the door, she couldn't quite shirk
    The realization that her boy was refraining
From his bitter-sweet begging her to stay home from work.
    He'd done no whining, no relentless complaining.
And though it made her feel sad not to feel the need
    Of her little boy begging that she stay,
She knew of no other way to both love and to feed,
    So, resigned, she started the car and drove away.

The little one was eager to start his brand-new day,
So he quickly drank his last bit of juice.
Looking up, he asked, "Whatcha readin', Gramps, what's it say?"
Grandpa answered, "Oh, I'm just reading the news.
And in today's world, the news is most never good.
Stories of wars tearing people apart.
Mostly bad things, people not bein' as they should.
It's a shame, but seems most people don't have a heart."

The little one frowned, not understanding what was said.
He asked, because he knew it couldn't be true,
"Grandpa, without a heart, wouldn't they be dead?"
The old man laughed, "That's enough questions out of you!
What's say we go out and really enjoy the day?
Let's look for that baseball!" he said with a wink.
"That sounds good to me, Gramps, but later, OK?
But right now, I think I just want to think."

"If you want," Grandpa replied, "But take my advice.
When I've got a lot to think about,
I go out on the porch, in the sun where it's nice,
And quiet. Make things easier to figure out."
So, they put on their coats and went outside.
The sun felt so good on their face.
They smelled the fresh air, breathed in deep inside.
They both smiled and gave the Spring a big embrace.

As they sat on the porch, the little boy thought
About the words that his Grandpa had spoken.
About the homeless, and God, and other things he taught,
And about his dad who had left his home broken.
Then he looked at the trees, where the breeze did rustle
The leaves that despite winter made it through.
And he felt the wind in his own hair tussle,
And at that moment, he knew exactly what he must do.

"Grandpa, Grandpa, I figured it out!
I know what I gotta do!
And you just might have to help me out,
A little, but I have to do it most, not you."
"Do what?" Grandpa questioned, totally confused
By the little boy's sudden outburst.
"What I promised last night," the small one mused.
"But, I gotta do som'pin' else, first"

"You stay here, Gramps," said the boy, running inside.
"I'll be back in a little while."
Then he got some paper and had to decide
On a color crayon, and in his own distinctive style,
He wrote at the table, a little poem,
Writing as neatly as he could:

DER GRAMPS -
TANK U 4
GIVEN ME N MOM
A HOM.
i NO LIVIN HER
WIL B GUD

(Dear Gramps, thank you for giving me and Mom a home.)
(I know living here will be good.)

A Dance of Light and Dark

All excited the little boy then ran out
To present Grandpa with his masterpiece.
At first, the old man couldn't figure it out,
But then it hit him, and he gave the boy a squeeze.
"This is beautiful, Little Guy, and you're very welcome!
How'd you learn to write so young, this way?"
"Well, Mommy taught me the letters and what they say some,
But I'm not sure, is my spellin' OK?

"It's perfect!" the old man said with a quiver,
I wouldn't have it any other way!"
The old man knew he'd keep the poem forever,
Forever 'til his dying day.
"Now Gramps, I need your help with som'pin' else,"
The boy whispered in a voice so contrite.
"'Cause I'm too little to do it myself,
So, would you please help me to make a kite?"

"Now how'd you know that I was a master kite maker?"
Grandpa laughed, "My kites never fail!
What we need is some sticks, glue, string and brown paper,
And rip up some rags for a beautiful long tail!"
Excited they both ran all around,
Collecting everything the project required.
And they built the kite together, strong and sound,
Its craftsmanship, truly inspired.

When done, they leaned the kite up against the wall
And stepped back to give a visual test.
The kite stood there, so majestic and tall
As it proudly thrust out its chest.
"Let's give it a try!" Grandpa said with a burst.
"Not yet, Gramps," was the young boy's remark.
"There's som'pin' I hafta write on it first,
And then I wanna take it down to the park.

"Now Gramps, I know you wanna play, but I got stuff ta get done!"
The boy chided, knowing full well his goals.
"So, you'll just hafta be patient, later we'll have fun!"
The old man laughed at the reversal of roles.
But keeping his laughter bottled up inside,
He said, "Well, sounds like you know what you want!"
And he watched as the boy and his kite did glide
Out of the kitchen on their little jaunt.

While waiting, he reread the boy's poem to himself
Several times, but the tyke soon returned.
"I really wanted ta do this all by myself!
I wish I knew everything!" he spurned.
"Mom said to be careful when she teached me each letter,
She said that some letters could sound kinda odd.
But I can't get this word, so I thought I better
Ask for your help. So, how do you spell God?"

Grandpa smiled at the tyke and said tenderly,
"Yeah, words can be tricky, and it's good that you ask.
You spell god like this, G-O-D."
The little one hurried back to his task.
The old man pondered, that though he employed all his powers,
All his anger, all his hate and all his fears,
That he'd thought about God more in the last twenty hours
than he had in the last twenty years.

The man felt resigned that this was so,
His soul frozen with his pain and despair.
Since god had forsaken him, why shouldn't he grow
Into a bitter old man who didn't care?
He had given up the quest of trying to answer
Questions of the Grand Scheme, or just why things occurred.
All of his anger and hatred had grown like a cancer
Making his vision of life numbed and blurred.

But, just as his torment was starting to build
To a point where he couldn't take anymore,
The winter in his soul was suddenly unchilled
As the little boy stormed through the door.
The old man was startled by the boy's sudden eruption,
And he wondered just how it was so
That this baby could wipe clean this old man's corruption.
The little one, excited yelled, "Let's go!"

"Now wait a second, my Little Crusader!"
Warned Gramps, trying to calm the boy down.
"But, Gramps, I told you that you could play later!
Well, Gramps, later's here! It's right now!
Feeling totally exhausted by his torment and despair
The old man took his time getting up.
"Patience, Little Guy! Do you see this gray hair?
That means I'm old, and tired, and all used up!"

"You're not old, Gramps. Nah, I don' think so!
Mom says you're just not used ta playin' n' havin' fun.
So, come on, Gramps! Hurry up! Let's go!
If you want, you can be old again when we're done.
So, Grandpa started to move a little bit faster,
Though he felt like a tired old hag,
For he knew he couldn't stand up to his little taskmaster.
Then he noticed that the kite was in a big bag.

"Trying to hide something from me, Little Guy?"
The little one turned red, and said as he giggled,
"I just want you to see it first, high in the sky!"
Growing impatient, the small one wiggled.
"Don't worry, Gramps, I didn't write nothin' bad on there,"
Said the boy, pulling on his Grampa's elbow.
It's just how I'm gonna tell people to care,
So, hurry up, Gramps, let's go!"

So, the two started off on their two-mile trek
Down the street to the park across town.
The little one carried the bag on his back,
But too big, it dragged along the ground.
The boy wasn't quite so excited now,
But determined and deep in thought.
Intent on keeping his promised vow,
Resolved to win the battle fought.

When they were half-way there, Grampa broke the silence,
Though he hesitated to interrupt
The small one's intensity, his total innocence,
So, he asked, not being judgmental or abrupt,
"Do you really think what you're doing will really make a change
In the way that people feel or think"
Cause, I just don't know, and you might think this strange,
But I'm afraid they'll ignore it, not even give it a blink!"

"Maybe we should turn around and go back to our place
And try out the kite first in our own backyard.
I'd hate so to see hurt on your little face
'Cause I know disappointment can be hard."
The small one listened carefully to everything he heard,
But he resented the introduction of the doubt.
So, he expressed with annoyance in every word –
"Grampa, that's som'pin I just can't think about!"

But, the little one recanted, fearing he'd been bad,
"Grampa, I know that you know lots of stuff,
And I know that you don't want me to be sad,
But 'bout my kite, ya just don't know enough,
Cause if'n you did, then you'd think I was right.
Maybe if I tell ya more about it, then you'll un'erstand."
And with that, he dismissed all his doubt outright
And the little boy kept walking – bag in hand.

A Dance of Light and Dark

The trees in the park came into view,
And from afar, they saw the wind sway their branches.
And the two walked along, totally subdued,
Each one in their own separate trances.
They entered the park and found a place to rest
Near the edge of a big, open grass field
The little boy determined to accomplish his quest;
The old man afraid of its yield.

The noonday sun had brought all in the town
Out of their winter-long hibernation.
They all wore its warmth on their heads like a crown
And each one gave the sun an ovation.
They had been waiting for this day like the frozen
Yearning to spring from the ground and flower.
They turned their faces to the sun in an act of selfish greed,
While enjoying their radiant lunch hour.

Squirrels gathering nuts ran all about
Trying to replenish their winter supply.
And robins flying in from the south
Began descending from the bright sky.
The boy, too, was anxious to get on with his mission,
But knew that before he began
That he'd have to first get his Grampa's permission
To fly his kite and to execute his plan.

"Gramps, ya told me las' night by the fireplace there
That ta help homeless people what I have ta do
Is to tell other people that they gotta care.
But that seemed way simple, way simple to do.
Cause if it was that simple, somebody'd already done it
And there wouldn't be homeless people anywhere!
So, I guess people don't care because they just don't wan'it.
And, how can people care if they don't care that they care?"

"But what you said this morning, Gramps, really got me ta think,
When you told me that most people don't have a heart.
That really mixed me up!" the boy paused, they said with a blink,
"You wouldn't say som'pin that dumb. You're too smart!
So, you must have meant som'pin in a different way.
Mommy does that sometimes, too.
I don' like it when grown-ups don' mean what they say!
Cause ya never know what you're s'possed ta do!"

"So, I thinked about just what ya really might a said
When we was on the porch, outside in the chair.
And then an idea just popped into my head!
It said, 'What Grampa means is that people don' care.'
I think that's what ya meant, Gramps, is it true?"
Amazed at the boy, Grampa could only nod his head.
"That was weird! Did ideas ever pop like that into you?"
The old man still gripped by silence, again nodded instead.

"But, that's what gave me the answer, Gramps!
When I figured that out, I knew just what to do!
Don' ya un'erstand what the answer was Gramps?"
The old man stammered, but somehow words came through.
"I'm sorry Little Guy, I want to understand.
Could you try a little harder to explain it to me?"
The boy rubbed Grampa's back with his tiny hand.
"I'll make you un'erstand, Gramps, you'll see."

"Ya see, to help the homeless, I hafta start
By tellin' people that they should care and give.
And if people care, then they'd have a heart,
Cause, without a heart, then where would God live?
People might not care if other people are homeless,
And I know that they really aren't right.
But I bet they _really_ care if they knew that God was homeless!
Whatta ya think, Gramps? I think they might!"

The old man was stunned by the boy's simple solution
To the problems all over the earth.
This child's message of caring could bring absolution
Of all the sins we've all had since birth.
He said, "Little Guy. How'd you ever get so wise?"
The little boy stopped thinking it through.
"It wasn't me." He finally said, looking his Gramps in the eyes.
"It didn't come from me, Gramps. I learned it from *you*!"

In total disbelief, the old man thought, "Could it be
That the answers were always locked deep inside?
And did this little, innocent child hold the key?"
The old man broke down and cried.
The little boy felt sorry to see the old man cry
And promised, "Don' worry Gramps, I won' be sad.
It don' matter if people laugh at my kite in the sky,
Cause if even just one person un'erstands, I'll be glad."

"And you know what else, Gramps? It just might be
That somebody here will see it and be less mad
And they just might help the homeless, and it just might be
That the homeless that they help – just might be my dad."
But, if ya still don' care to fly my kite, Gramps, I'll un'erstand.
We can go home right now and not never try it."
But, the old man reached inside with all the strength he could
command

And yelled a whisper, "I care, Little Guy! Let's fly it!"
So, hand in hand they walked onto the field,
The warm breeze was blowing through their hair.
The boy carried the bag within the kite safely sealed.
They both looked around at the hundreds gathered there.
"Now, Gramps," the tyke reminded, "don' you look at my kite
Til it's flying way high in the air."
The old man smiled at the boy and said, "all right,
I won't look. I promise Little Guy."

31

The little boy then carefully unsealed the sack
And pulled out the kite tail and all.
And he handed it to the old man, only seeing its back
Then started unraveling his little string ball.
Walking backwards with the string, the boy watched the sight
Of his Grampa with the kite ready to throw.
Then he yelled to the crowd, "Hey everybody! Watch my kite!"
Followed by the old man shouting "Let's go!"

The little boy ran as fast as he could.
His Gramps threw the kite way up high.
The kite shot up like a rocket ship would.
Soon the boy stopped and admired it in the sky.
He let out some slack, so it flew over his Gramps head,
Then he let out more, so its message he wouldn't miss.
And the old man looked up at the kite, which said:

[Please care – Don't let God be homeless.]

A Dance of Light and Dark

"Oh no!" the old man thought. "No one will get it! The boy will fail!"
And thoughts of his own failures came boiling to the top.
"I can't let this happen! I can't let pain prevail!"
And was just about to tell the boy to stop...
But then he saw the look of hope on the little boy's face,
And remembered that the boy had measured his success
By the understanding of just one person at that place.
He then knew who that one person was.

There in the sun, the old man could feel himself melt,
Somehow now understanding his life, as it were.
And he could barely now feel all the pain that he felt,
And he knew what caused his heart to stir.
He said aloud, "Yeah, winter's been a really rough one this year."
And then he cheered for the boy and his kite.
It was apparent that life would soon persevere.
Winter's death-grip was losing the fight.

By Jerry L Style

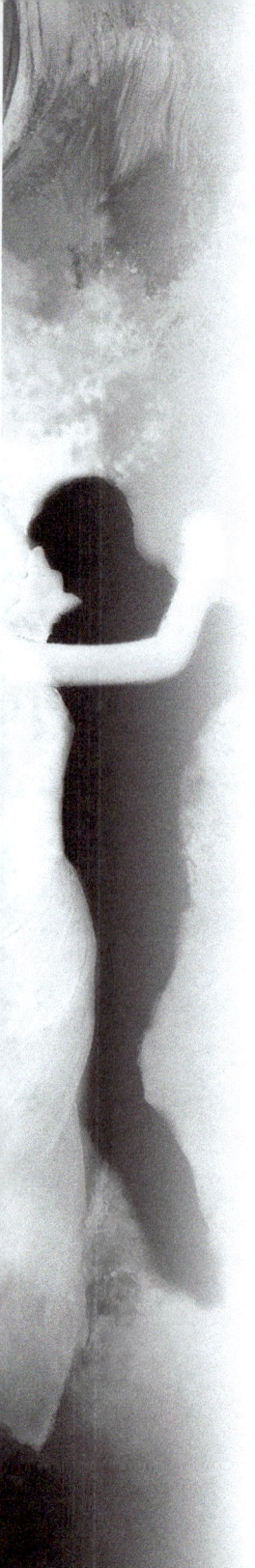

Happiness Is a Mom

When I was just a little girl
Maybe six or seven
I wrote my mom a poem
Because to me, she was heaven

"Happiness Is a Mom"
Was what I titled it
And even to this day
That title is still a fit

I wrote about the things
She always let me do
Like keeping frogs and turtles
When most moms would say eww

She let me iron the handkerchiefs
One of my many joys
I know that sounds crazy
But for me, better than toys

She was happy to forgive me
When Leslie James and I
Fell into the creek
And came home wet, not dry

She let me be a brownie
The girl scout kind of fun
And she would come and get me
When music class was done

Happy was so easy then
The little joys we tell
And as I grew older
The happiness did as well

A Dance of Light and Dark

Happiness is a mom
Who always makes me smile
She listens so intently
Because that's just her style

We love to make the brownies
These, the kind you eat
All chocolatey warm and gooey
Such a special treat

We love to plant the garden
Flowers and veggies galore
And had the deer not eaten them
Tulips were in store

Happiness is a mom
Who celebrates every win
And inspires all her children
To dive back in again

Happiness is a mom
Who loves so long and deep
She kept that poem for 60 years
Then gave back to me to keep

So on this special birthday
At 95 years strong
Like the first poem said
Happiness is just having a mom

By Anne Pollard
April 17, 2024

Truth

by jerry l style

BeL**I**Eve Me!

Explanation
(Reading from top to bottom)
I LIE Believe Me!
This is a conundrum.

What is the author trying to say?

The reader has a choice to believe the author or not.

If the author lies as he claims that he does, <u>and</u> if you believe him, then the statement that "I lie" would therefore be a lie, and is therefore a statement of truth.

If the author lies as he claims that he does, <u>and</u> you do NOT believe him, then the statement "I lie" is in fact a statement of truth.

Either way you look at it, it is a truth statement.

My Power

I see my power

For it is within that power that unconditional love abides in

I awaken my power

For it is within that power that I see the beauty of earth, fire, water and wind

I take back my power

For it is within that power that I create the reality I want to live in

I honor my power

For it is within that power that I transform myself and ascend

I STAND IN MY POWER

For it is within that power that I am the light, even through the end

By Anne Pollard

After the Storm

After the storm, the wind – now a breeze
Causes the smooth and relaxing sound
Of the raindrops being caught up high in the trees
Now falling off and softly hitting the ground.

After the storm, distant lightning silhouettes
Far off hills, now just echoing thunder
Of battles that were waged over future regrets,
Of the stresses we both were under.

After the storm, is the time realized
That this is the moment we've wished for
While we waited with futures so jeopardized,
While we hoped to have peace once more.

After the storm, we reflect likelihood
Of how we'd feel with the life that we had.
Would we ever be feeling so now very good
If we never had felt so very bad?

After the storm, bad memories will pale
And over time become distant past.
And the feelings for each other will always prevail
And this calming bliss will forever last.

By Jerry L Style

In The Flow

Wow, I'm in the flow!
But how do you know?

Synchronicities happen, again and again
If I Yang, then I Yen

I'm really in the flow!
Yeah, but how do you know?

The people I meet are drawn to me
And I'm inspired with creativity

I'm feeling the flow!
But how do you know?

When I want to have some fun
The sky is always full of sun

I *am* the flow!
Still, how do you know?

The path ahead is just so clear
And because of that, I have no fear

I want to know how I can be in the flow!

Oh, it's easy you see
Just release and let go
Trust and be free
Then, just KNOW!

By Anne Pollard

Don't wake me up

Lying here, next to you,
Held softly in your embrace,
I feel your breath, I feel its steam,
I feel your body warm me up.
But I wonder, is this real? Is it true?
Am I really at this place?
Or is this just some wonderful dream?
If it is, then please don't wake me up.

Let me dream my life on in sensual sleep,
Let me keep these hallucinations.
Let fantasy live on, let desires persist,
In this blissful, unconscious coverup.
Will night dreams be seared in my memory deep?
Were all these unreal fascinations?
Were those your tender lips last night that I kissed?
If they weren't, please don't wake me up.

Now, the experts all say
Not to live life this way,
That the real world is where we all should stay.
But if in the light of day
There isn't any other way,
Then I'd rather dream my whole life away.

Sure, I hope that all of this is real,
And hope that I have been awake,
I hope for more and more and more.
I hope that life passes its reality check-up.
But if the truth will finally reveal
That my life has all been a fake,
Then to dream is all I have in store,
If that's true, then please don't wake me up.

By Jerry L Style

Playing the Quantum Field

The musical matrix before my eyes
A vision of infinite lines
Keys to The Universe in the skies
The Quantum Field aligns

I pluck each string with fingers strong
The Universe plays the base
The sound combines in epic song
A symphony in place

Infinite joy awaits the soul
The rhythm pushes faster
More lines shift to meet my goal
The field is now the master

Co-create for higher good
The music then evolves
My higher soul now takes the reigns
The Quantum Field responds

It sings a song of all as one
        More souls join the matrix
And thus the field expands again
        And consciousness awakens

The melody plays of past and future
        Although there's no such thing
It all happens simultaneously
        Within the Quantum ring

The field knows neither time nor space
        It's energy at its core
It's everywhere, not just one place
        The Quantum Field is more

A trillion songs now join the chorus
        The music from above
And all will blend in perfect voices
        The Quantum Field of love

By Anne Pollard

This is a song written about Hurricane Irma as it battered the islands of St Thomas and St. John. St John is also known as Love City.

Love City

With just you in my dreams
Let's go down where it seems
That the island music never will stop.
Where our love cannot fail
And the winds in our sail
Blow us to the highest **Mountain Top**.
Sea turtles still graze
Under **Cruz and Trunk Bays**
And the sunsets are still very pretty
The palm trees still sway
Next to **Cinnamon Bay**.
Make my dreams come true at **Love City**.

With just you in my prayers
Whether no one else cares,
There's still an island paradise.
Where the waters are blue
Where our dreams can come true
And the locals there are so very nice.
The corals still grow
Under **Hurricane Hole**
And the **Cruzan** is still cold and ready.
Waves still lap the shore
On **Bolongo** and more.
Won't you answer my prayers at **Love City**.

With just you in my heart
We will get a new start
We'll rebuild the dreams we had way back then.
Though damaged by storm
We soon will transform
And build another **Love** much stronger again.
Eagle rays still fly
Through the waters nearby.
And **Sapphire Beach** is still oh so pretty.
The soft wind still blows,
There's still sand in our toes.
Fill my heart with your love at **Love City**.

With just you in my arms
We'll renew all those charms,
We can soon be in heaven once more.
It's all within reach
Just like **Maho Bay** beach,
We'll embrace there again on the shore.
Our hearts will be filled
With the **Love** we'll rebuild
Don't you see it's almost there already?
Come join with me now
And I'll show you how.
Walk with me arm in arm in **Love City**.
Won't you answer my prayers…
Make my dreams come true…
Help rebuild our new **Love** – ----- – **Love City**.

By Jerry L Style

Timeless Love

Their love would last for decades
Seven, to be exact
Through all the ups and downs
That love, always intact

They lived through war and scarcity
But learned to work as one
Their love continued blooming
And soon they had a son

As he grew up, their parents died
Circle of life did swirl
But love remained around them
And soon they had a girl

Working hard to make ends meet
Their supportive love grew more
And blessed with one more child
Their future now instore

"I think we need a home" he said
And certainly, she agreed
From the dirt then rose a house
But became a home indeed

Sometimes there was strife
And some disharmony
But ultimately love prevails
For the sake of family

Years moved on; the kids grew up
With families of their own
The parents now grandparents
And another decade would dawn

Now sharing the support they could
A different kind of love
Sacrifice for the family
So they could rise above

The pets were always there as well
The dogs were splendid fun
They came and went as decades pass
Bringing love to this union

The grand kids grew and married to
Bringing great grandchildren now
The couple proud of legacy built
And more love to allow

As the final decade comes
They can both now look back
On a loving life well lived
And memories they can track

The bodies age over the years
And time moves quickly on
And even when they are back to spirit
This Timeless Love beams strong

By Anne Pollard

Timeless Love Complete

His arm reached down
From heaven above
Offering his hand
To his one true love

He promised he'd come
Sending her signs
The missing ring
Now she can find

She laid down that night
Dreamt of the day
When he would come for her
And whisk her away

He left before
She could go with him
But the time had come
For separation to end

Her preparation
Was sealed all the same
Nothing remained
In playing the game

It happened quite gently
Her choice was so clear
To be with her husband
And leave with no fear

Her spirit ascended
To unconditional love
Embraced by all consciousness
She was so worthy of

Her family was there
Eager for closure
The parents, the sister,
Even Lillie Moser

The pets awaited
Tails wagging fast
They missed her as well
Oh, to see her at last!

The reunion was grand
In light they did meet
This Timeless Love
Now forever complete

By Anne Pollard

The Gift

The city lay frozen in the desolate night air,
On a frigid and heartless Valentine's Eve.
The bitter cold air left nothing but despair.
Without warmth and light, life seemed only make believe.
The cold night chill blew through every dark street
As it mindlessly pushed around yesterday's news.
But Winter knew it was futile, for it could not compete
Against the sun, for within hours – it would certainly lose.

But its time was now, and Winter knew that it must
Reign in terror as long as it could
Be a power of darkness, greed and lust
And trample anything with even a trace of good.
So, it revved up its winds and pounded the city
With a powerful show of brute force,
Sending wind and snow down without mercy or pity,
Causing death and destruction without a hint of remorse.

The buildings of the city, like sullen tombstones
Trembled from the clout of the violent rage.
The shaken buildings emitted painful creaks and groans
As Winter added dozens of years to their age.
All the lights were all out, electricity gone
As residents scurried for the strength to cope.
And in a fourth story window burned a lone
Candle flickering as a desperate sign of last hope.

For hours the storm ravaged on, hell-bent,
Pounding what life in the streets still remained.
But at last, Winter's powers were fully spent
Leaving behind a city all broken and maimed.
Cautiously people began to emerge
From their homes, relieved to be alive.
And residual winds sounded a mournful dirge
For those victims of the rage who had failed to survive.

The sun began rising in the dreary haze
As if ashamed to be too little too late.
And the light that it shed revealed a shocking gaze
Of the carnage and ruin left in Winter's wake.
Trees littered streets like broken toothpicks.
Fractured windows had thrown glass all around.
Frozen refuse was scattered about ankle thick
Making bizarre designs of trash on the ground.

Men and women and their families, too
Began cleaning the littered landscape.
Afraid of Winter's angry return, they knew
That they needed a clear path for a potential speedy escape.
So, spite the cold, a little girl carried a bagful of debris
Down the alley to the waste bin out back,
She whistled and danced to be finally free
Of the prison caused by Winter's brutal attack.

As the girl skipped along, she kicked a can,
Feeling great that she was again free to play.
But the alley was strewn with frozen contraband,
With crates and boxes blocking the way.
So, the girl began clearing a path
To the waste bin now just yards away,
Pushing boxes aside, rearranging Winter's wrath,
Restoring order to the storm's disarray.

As she worked her way to clear the ground,
A single large box blocked her approach.
The box lay stubborn, completely icebound,
Resisting all of her efforts to reproach.
But when she looked down, her eyes filled with fear
And uncontrollably, she let out a loud yelp,
For from under the box, so painfully near
Was a frozen hand reaching up, begging for help.

At first, the girl was stunned, unable to flee,
Overcome by the sight of the gruesome scene.
Then she finally ran through the trash and debris
Hysterically crying scream after terrorized scream,
She ran blindly out into the street
Into the arms of patrolling cops.
Frightfully, she pointed down toward the concrete,
Hardly able to speak through all of her sobs.

The girl's mom came out to take her inside,
And the police drew their guns in defense.
Then carefully, they crept down the alley, side by side,
Ever watchful, alert and intense.
They'd been down this alley many times before,
Not for crooks wielding a gun or a knife,
But for vagrants, homeless or an occasional whore
Looking for shelter or a place to escape from life.

They neared the end of the alley, and warily spied
The box that the girl told them was there
She had seen the frozen hand reaching up from the side
Of the box labelled "Handle With Care."
While one officer stood posed with his gun
The other kicked over the crate.
Under the box was a lifeless, frozen bum;
For him, help had come far too late.

The homeless man looked to be about age thirty,
Though it was easy to think he'd be much older.
His eyes were frozen open, his face dank and dirty.
He had drunk bottles of rum as the weather got colder.
His clothes were all torn, shoes all battered,
His face was a strange purple gray.
His was a life that just never mattered,
So, society had simply tossed it away.

Oddly, the man's face showed no emotion,
No anger, frustration or fears.
And his cheeks were caved in, revealing the notion
That he hadn't had a good meal for many, many years.
The police searched the man's pockets for some sort of ID,
But they found only a picture, torn and frayed,
Of a woman with a small boy sitting on her knee.
Sadly, one cop sighed, "Happy Valentine's Day."

They radioed headquarters to send a hearse
To remove the frozen body from its impersonal tomb.
And they hauled it away, cleansing the curse
From the streets, this unwanted picture of gloom.
Following their familiar routine by the book,
They took the man's picture and fingerprints.
But, once the file was closed, it wouldn't get another look;
Like ocean wave erasing a beach's footprints.

The body was placed in a casket made of pine
And trucked to a plot that all else had rejected.
The labeled the gravesite, "John Doe #959,"
Joining others that society had neglected.
There was no clergy there to give the last rites,
No Psalm Twenty-Three, not even a prayer.
As if even death could not relieve the man's plights.
As if even in Heaven, there'd be no one to care.

The grave was then filled with frozen chunks of dirt
That the diggers did their best to smooth down.
And in the rest of the cemetery, weeds tried to convert
The scarred landscape from looking so bleak and brown.
Within months, the sun strengthened and warmed the earth,
And wild flowers began dutifully spreading their seeds
To the barren grave site, hungry for birth
And it began to sprout magnificent weeds.

A Dance of Light and Dark

Soon the sepulcher wore a beautifully flowered mask
Where birds and bees hovered in search of nectar.
For Mother Nature had fulfilled a dual task
To protect innocent eyes from the forsaken specter
Of a landscape reserved for the unwanted dead.
But more urgent, she brought back to life with abundance
A section of ground which the world had rejected
Resurrecting life from the plague of indifference.

For though life may be scarred by vicious assaults
It has a much stronger resolve.
And no matter the pain, the final results
Are that life will prolong and evolve.
For darkness is merely the absence of light,
And cold, the absence of heat.
Their strength is not measured in terms of their might,
But by the degree that their counterparts are in retreat.

One month later, and a thousand miles away
An old man and small boy were playing ball in the yard.
Enjoying to the fullest, spring's first pleasant day,
The old man warned, "Now don't swing too hard!
"Just watch the ball hit your bat,
And I promise that you'll get a hit."
So, the little boy, outfitted in his brand-new hat
Stood there, bat cocked, a picture of true grit.

The old man threw the ball towards the cardboard home plate
And the boy studied the orb in its flight.
He bit his lower lip and felt his blood pulsate
As he swung the bat with all of his might.
The tyke's powerful swing spun him completely around
As the baseball flew safely passed.
Grampa laughed at the boy, sprawled on the ground
But the little boy got up lightning fast.

"Pitch it again, Gramps," cried the little guy
As he ran back to retrieve the ball.
"I know I can hit it if I really try!"
And he resumed his stance straight and tall.
"Now, sometimes it's better if you try just a bit,"
Said Gramps, trying to instill some control.
"Now don't swing too hard, and you'll get a hit.
Now remember – just watch the ball!"

Again, Grampa tossed the ball at the strike zone,
But again, the boy swung overly hard.
And again, the little guy ended up prone,
And again, he picked himself up off the yard.
Time after time, the boy took a mighty swing,
And time after time he'd miss.
Finally, Grampa said, "Let me tell you something,
Because you just can't go on like this!"

"You see, Little Guy, sometimes it's best
Not to try with all of your might,
Because some things are harder to do than the rest,
So, rather than doing it hard, do it right.
Now, I'm going to stand here nice and close
And throw the ball to you nice and slow,
And you just try to hit it, but not over the house.
Just meet the ball, I promise it will go!"

"All right, Gramps, I'll give it a try,"
Said the lad as he resumed his stance.
And again, Gramps let the ball fly
To the boy, anxious for his next chance.
Suddenly, the quiet spring air was filled
With a resounding crack of a wooden bat,
And the ball sailed upward, the little boy shrilled
And danced around like an acrobat.

"Run!" Grampa shouted, "Run to first base!"
And the old man chased after the ball.
The little guy ran around all over the place,
Laughing and dancing, trying not to fall.
The old man picked up the ball near the fence,
"Run Home!" he yelled with an excited burst
As the little boy grew determined at the suspense
Of who would get to home plate first.

The little boy ran as fast as he could
And his Gramps took off in the chase,
But in an instant the old man new that he would
Beat the tenacious little boy to home base.
So, while the boy wasn't looking, he paused for a bit
To give the little guy a fighting chance.
And although the small one grew tired, he couldn't quit
From making his home plate advance

As the little guy got close, he took a great dive
Toward home plate just ahead of the tag.
"You're Out!" Grampa laughed, feigning to deprive
The Little Slugger from his chance to brag.
"I'm safe!" the boy protested. "I'm SAFE! I REALLY AM!"
"All right, Little Guy, you were safe. A HOME RUN!"
"YES!" cried the boy, "What a hit!" whooped the man.
And the two rolled around, reveling in their fun.

As the merry two frolicked around on the ground
The little boy's mom arrived home from work.
She felt great to be home, safe and sound
From her thankless job as a grocery clerk.
"Hi guys!" she yelled as she opened the car door.
"I've got pizza! Come on in. Let's eat!"
"HURRAY!" cried the boy, for there was nothing he loved more
Than pizza, so he quickly jumped to his feet.

He ran to his mom and gave her an energetic hug,
Surprising her at the burst of affection.
Then he grabbed grocery bags and began to lug
Them to the house, giving them a complete inspection.
"And ice cream!" he cheered. "What a great day!"
And the three scurried through the fence gate.
They sat at the table, paused to pray.
Gramps placed some pizza on everyone's plate.

"So, tell me all about this great day of yours."
Said mom as she lifted her glass to drink.
The boy quickly choked down his pizza before
He responded, "Best day of my life, I think!
What d'ya think, Gramps, I think I'm right!"
Then he excitedly babbled like a bustling machine gun,
"We went out on the porch, I had an idea, we made a kite,
Flew it at the park to help the homeless, and... I HIT A HOME
RUN!"

Mom laughed, "Whoa! Slow down! Not so fast, my child!
Your mouth is sayin' words faster than my ear can hear!"
So, knowing he had to calm down, the boy smiled
And playfully said, "all right, Mother dear,
I'll slow down, but ya better lissen close,
Cause so much happened today, that I just might forget it.
But I promise that I'll try to tell you most
Of what happened, so just relax and don't sweat it!"

Grampa scolded the boy, "Don't you talk that way
To your mom, you must treat her nice!
And besides, looks like she's had a very long day.
So, maybe you'll just have to say some things twice."
So, the boy apologized to his weary mom
And restarted talking about his eventful day.
"Well, it started when me 'n Gramps were talkin 'bout home,
'N the homeless, 'n Daddy, 'n why he ran away."

A Dance of Light and Dark

Immediately, mom shot a worried look
At the old man across the table.
It was a look that the little boy seldom mistook.
An expression of fear that he tried to disable.
"Don' worry, Mom. Gramps didn't say nothin' bad 'bout you,
Or 'bout me, or 'bout himself, neither.
He just said that Daddy was mixed up and confused,
But he didn't say nothin' bad 'bout Daddy, neither."

"But, since Daddy ran away, then he must be homeless.
Grampa said that there were people like that everywhere.
'N when I asked Gramps just why some people were homeless,
He told me that it was 'cause most people just don' care."
The little boy took another slice of pizza pie.
Grampa sat there in silence, but the day's memories brought
A tear of happiness to the old man's eyes.

Mom knew from the look on the two guys faces
That something happened that day quite profound.
"Grampa's right, you know. There should be more places
Where the homeless could go to be safe and sound."
"I know that, Mom," the little boy said
"But today, I thought somepin' else.
It was weird, cause an idea just popped into my head,
Like it didn' even come from myself!"

"Ya see, I figured that there weren' 'nough people who
Care, so they don't have a heart.
But then I thought, 'I'm a people, too,'
So, since I had the idea, I'd hafta start.
So, I asked Grampa to help me make somepin'
That lotsa people would see and be glad.
'Cause I hoped when they saw it, they'd do sompin'
To help homeless people, and maybe even my Dad!"

59

"You wait, here, Mom, 'cause I want ya ta take a look
At what we did. Be right back, all right?"
The boy went over to the closet, and took
Out a splendid, though wind-battered kite.
The boy took the kite, held it high over his head
As he stood there proudly, a vision of success.
And Grampa and Mom looked up at the kite which said

"What cha think, Mom, do ya know what it meant?"
Mom took a few seconds to figure it out,
"I think so," she said, impressed at the scene
Of the boy and his kite, though she still had some doubt.
"I think it means that people should care,
'cause that's what God wants them to do."
"Well, that's Kinda right," he said, now back in his chair,
"But not quite, so I guess I'll explain it to you."

"Remember, Mom, when you told me that
You think God lives in your heart?
Well, that mornin', Grampa told me that
If people don' care, then they don' have a heart.
So, people have ta care, 'cause if'n they don't,
Then God wouldn't have a place to stay.
So I tried ta tell people to care so God won't
Be homeless and lonely that way."

The little boy's mom was overcome with emotion
By his loving display, so kind and humane.
For she had dedicated her life to the love and devotion
Of her family, but 'til now, it'd just been a drain.
The love she gave her husband had never been returned,
But she gave and she gave 'til she had nothing left.
But her husband only took and spitefully spurned
Her love, leaving her alone and bereft.

Instantly, her mind was filled with the frustration
That she had experienced during those years of despair.
A frustration so deep that it led to the creation
Of the belief that it just didn't pay to care.
But, there at the table she saw her son through her tears,
And then realized that, though misdirected,
That her loving and caring through all of those years
Bounced off her husband to her son, as though divinely reflected.

The old man sat there, equally mute,
For today after suffering many years of blight,
The life in his heart was suddenly renewed
By the innocent little boy and his kite.
For in the many years of the old man's life
He'd been kicked around by frustration and despair.
All the fighting with his son, and the death of his wife
Led him, too, to the belief that he just should not care.

For years he had assumed the self-imposed blame
Even though he had tried with all of his might,
That his efforts as a father and husband brought only shame.
That he hadn't done enough. He hadn't done it right.
But that day as he watched the little boy at the park
The chains of his despair had been all but shattered.
And his life no longer seemed so dismal and dark.
For he realized the one thing that really mattered.

Breaking the silence, the small boy said, "Then we went
To the park. There were lots 'n lots a people there.
But, d'ya think anyone understood what my kite meant?"
Grampa responded, "I know they did, Little Guy, I swear!"
"Well, I hope so," pensively the little boy sighed.
But then his thoughtful mood was suddenly undone.
"And then we came home and played baseball outside,
And then, guess what, Mom! I hit a HOME RUN!"

Mom didn't know whether to laugh or cry,
So, she did a little bit of each.
Smiling through her tears, she said, "You're quite a guy!"
Then she rose from the table to give her son a squeeze.
And, knowing full well that the old man had
Much to do with her son's thoughtful analysis,
She went to the man, and smiling said, "Thanks, Dad,"
Leaned over and gave him a kiss.

A Dance of Light and Dark

The old man was embarrassed at the show of affection,
For it was the first time that anyone had called him "dad."
"You're welcome, but I just answered his questions."
Then, tongue-tied by emotion, he had nothing more to add.
But he stuttered, "I best go outside and gather some wood.
Another storm's coming tonight, maybe the year's worst.
Mom smiled, "I love the fire, but Little Guy we should
Clean up the kitchen and take a bath first."

So, Mom and the boy straightened up after dinner,
Then they went upstairs to clean up.
Grampa put on his coat and ventured out into winter
Where the storm's winds were already starting to pick up.
The sun had set as if acting on cue,
Winter again, began its vicious onslaught.
The sky had turned a strange purple black and blue,
Gathering its strength for the battle to be fought.

The old man looked up at the storm with awe,
Amazed at the strength of the powerful force.
And he marveled at how fast the sun could withdraw
To be replaced by shear devastation and discourse.
Dark clouds rolled in like a huge tidal wave
As they crashed down on earth's fragile beaches.
And the darkness they cast would make even the brave
Run for cover midst screams and screeches.

In an instant, the dark winter skies opened wide,
Sending down torrents of snow and ice.
The old man hurried to get back inside,
As the stinging sleet pelted his frost-bitten face.
Back inside with the wood, the old man shook,
Not knowing whether from the cold or the fright,
He removed his drenched coat, and somberly looked
At the dripping wood, wondering if it would light.

The old man put the soaked wood in the hearth,
Carefully adding some extra kindling.
He noticed that the storm had made the house dark
And that the temperature was quickly dwindling.
So, he lit the fire in several places
And fanned it gently to nurse it along.
But the wet wood was stubborn, giving the old man traces
Of doubt that he'd get the fire going.

The old man crinkled up some old newspaper
And introduced it to the struggling fire.
It slowly started to grow, emitting steam and vapor
As it tried to relieve the wood from its icy mire.
But the flames required repeated cajoling
For the man knew that if left unattended,
That darkness and cold would end up controlling,
And the fire's short life would be suddenly ended.

The boy and his mom then entered the room,
All neat and clean and ready for bed.
Expecting the fire's warmth and its sweet perfume,
But disappointed, they snuggled under a blanket instead.
"There's quite a storm, tonight," Grampa reported,
"And the wood's wet and frozen and hard to light."
The fire hiss, and defiantly spit and snorted,
As it, too, gathered its strength for the fight.

As the three sat in front of the struggling blaze,
The flames licked an ice-covered log.
But the dripping water just tried to betray
The fire from accomplishing its job.
As a result, the cold was reluctant to leave the room,
And the darkness unwilling to vanish.
As if they had a diabolical scheme of gloom
To extinguish the fire, and forever its power banish.

But the fire braved on, and developed a foothold,
And the old man seemed done with his laborious chore.
But suddenly, the room seemed to grow cold
As there was an unexpected heavy knocking at the door.
"Who could that be?" Grampa wondered out loud,
As he walked over to answer the knock.
And when he opened the door, he grew white as a shroud
Like experiencing a life-threatening shock.

A policeman stood there, dripping with ice.
The old man immediately invited him in.
The officer entered, introduced himself twice,
And asked if the little boy's mother was in.
He refused to answer the old man's questions when
Asked to explain the reason that he came.
So, the old man led him into the den
And the officer asked the boy's mother her name.

The policeman then stood at complete attention,
Very official, proper and sleek.
But his voice had a touch of cautious apprehension
As he cleared his throat and began to speak.
"The City Police regret to relay
That on February 14th, your husband was discovered
Frozen to death in an abandoned alley
Where he had tried to live in a cardboard box for cover.

The Mayor of the City offers his sympathy,
And information about the body can be found
By contacting City Hall between nine and three."
Then he paused, and timidly looked down.
"Well, if you don't mind, I really must go.
The storm's getting worse, no doubt
I have to return to the station in the snow,
But don't get up. I'll let myself out."

And with that, the officer left,
Having quickly told his tale of gloom.
The three just sat there, speechless and bereft,
As a dark presence seemed to inhabit the room.
They all felt the life flowing from their veins
When the officer was saying his piece.
Unable to move, feeling like earthly remains,
Passionless, lifeless, losing life's lease.

The den had been transformed into a lifeless morgue,
Where even the fire dimmed in its disgrace.
And after an eternity of motionlessness, the first thing that moved
Was a single tear rolling down the little boy's face.
The room was totally silent and hushed,
As if it would be useless to convey
Any sound to deaf ears, emotionally crushed,
Until Mom mournfully murmured, "On Valentine's Day."

Paralyzed with grief, and hardly breathing,
The old man had been frozen, life's hope deprived
But, suddenly he heard his heart faintly beating,
And, amazed, he realized that he was alive.
The sound of Mom's voice was like a slap in the face
That revived him out of his emotional coma,
And he realized that he was not alone in that place,
That the others, too, endured the frigid sarcoma.

"I'm so sorry," the old man sadly relented,
"I know that you both feel so sad,
But it's not your fault, for only I could have prevented
This dreadful event if I had been a better dad.
I don't know what I could have done different,
And I really tried with all of my might,
But all of my efforts did nothing to prevent
This tragedy, because I just didn't do it right."

66

A Dance of Light and Dark

The old man's words reminded the lad
Of something that he had wanted to confess.
So, he said, "Ya know, Gramps, ya shouldn't feel bad,
'Cause I know you tried hard and did your best.
Like today, remember when I was swingin' the bat
And I just kept missin' 'cause I swung too hard?
Ya told me not ta do it like that,
But I just couldn't stop doin' it hard!"

"Even when I hit the home run I did it
I was just lucky, I guess that way.
But no matter how hard I tried to swing slow and just hit it,
I just couldn't do it any other way."
The old man knew full well what the little boy meant,
That although he may have failed, at least he tried.
And it felt so good to receive the acknowledgement,
"From the mouths of babes," he quietly sighed.

"But, there's somepin' else I just don' get,"
Continued the boy with a frown on his face.
"I know that we're supposed to care, but yet,
It doesn't seem ta get ya anyplace.
'Cause I know that I cared 'bout my Dad,
And I know that you and Mommy did, too.
But it didn't help, 'cause now my Daddy's dead.
My kite didn't do what I wanted it to do!"

"So, I don' get it, Gramps, why should I care anymore?
It didn't do nothin' that I can see!
I don' think I wanna care anymore,
'Cause it just makes me sad. Can you explain it to me?"
The old man had to look away from the boy,
And he searched his mind for the reasons to try.
But all his hopes and dreams had also been destroyed.
He could only whisper, "I just don't know, Little Guy."

"I do," said Mom, "I found out the other night
When I read it for the first time myself.
I was cleaning my closet, when up near the light
I found a book hidden up on the shelf."
Then turning to the old man, she penitently said,
"It was your wife's diary, and I read all of it.
I'm sorry, I know I should've given it to you, instead
But is seemed that something powerful made me read it."

Mom left the room and came back with the book.
Its cover was worn and tattered.
And holding the diary, she gave the man a loving look.
"It's an amazing story of how your lives were shattered.
It tells how your days were filled with frustration
About your wanting children, but being denied,
And about adopting your son and its gay jubilation,
And about his autism, and how you cried."

"It tells about how you worked so hard
To provide for your wife and son,
But it also tells how your life had been scarred
By bad breaks that shouldn't happen to anyone.
But, there's one part that answers your question, Little Guy,
Let me read it, and you listen to what Gramma said."
Then, Mom opened the book, and trying not to cry
Pausing to wipe away her tears, she then read.

"I'm sorry to admit that my faith has been shaken
By the hardships we've had year-after-year.
And I know that I run the risk of being forever forsaken,
But I have serious doubts that God is still here.
Because if He were here, then how could He allow
All the pain that we've had in our life?
And I just don't know how He could possibly disavow
His responsibility for this agony and strife."

68

A Dance of Light and Dark

"Yet, maybe if I don't focus on the chaos,
But, instead on just what's important;
Maybe to think what could be, and not what was,
We might be able to stop the imminent descent
Of our lives from sinking into the sea of despair,
Where waves of remorse reach up to pull us down.
Maybe, to be positive, to love, to care,
We won't have to sink into that sea and drown."

"Yet, for me, it's too late, my life all but through,
But for my husband and son, there might be a chance.
I know they could make it if they focused on what's true,
Instead of on their own dire circumstance.
But it's my husband I worry mostly about.
He's such a good man, no one's ever tried more.
A dedicated husband and father, strong and devout,
But feeling inadequate by all pain that life bore."

"And my son, oh my son, never able to feel
All the love we were so anxious to give.
Always angry and resentful, I'm so afraid that he'll
Never truly know what it means to live.
For living and loving go hand in hand,
You can't have one without the other.
But this is something I'm afraid he'll never understand,
And without love, I know he won't even bother.

But I guess even though God may not be here, now,
I believe he once was, and that before he left,
He left something behind, something to endow
Us remaining on Earth, He gave us a gift.
This gift is unlike anything else,
Unlike anything else I can think of.
It's not wrapped in pretty paper with ribbons and bells.
No… the gift is pure, unadulterated love.

And the thing about this gift that's so strange
Is that no one can hoard it, or hide it away.
No, to accept this gift, a person must change,
For in order to receive it, it must be given away.
But even the giving can sometimes be hard,
Sometimes, it's not accepted, no matter how hard you try.
But you just can't stop trying, for you can't disregard
That if you don't give it away, your own love will die."

The little boy listened carefully
To each word that his mother had read.
And the old man clung to each word tearfully,
Almost believing he was hearing his wife's voice, instead.
Mom closed the book, her voice weak and contrite,
"That's the last thing she wrote," she said quietly,
And the boy looked at the fire, now burning bright,
And whispered, "Thanks, Gramma for explain that to me."

The little boy's words unleashed a flood of emotion,
And the three fell together, they cried, they hugged, they kissed.
For they knew that despite all the chaos and commotion,
That they'd prevail, for they knew that they all had the gift.
Without words, they consoled, and accepted each-others' caring,
And without shame each one was eager to requite.
They basked in the warmth of their loving and their sharing,
And clearly saw the gift in the glow of its light.

For though life may be scarred by vicious assaults
It has a much stronger resolve.
And no matter the pain, the final results
Are that life will prolong and evolve.
For darkness is merely the absence of light,
And cold, the absence of heat.
Their strength is not measured in terms of their might,
But by the degree that their counterparts are in retreat.

By Jerry L Style

When Did You Stop Singing?

Oh my sweet friend
Something is wrong, you agonize
I can see it in your eyes
Has something happened
Can we stop and chat
When did you stop singing?

I'm here for you
To listen and learn
Maybe I can help you discern
The nature of what's troubling you
Help you see you have a friend
When did you stop dancing?

You have support all around
Animal spirits, celestial guides
They envelop you on all sides
To bring you peace
To bring you love
When did you stop wondering?

71

It's OK to feel disjointed
We are humans with emotion
But also higher self devotion
Remember you are of divine
And that can never disappear
When will you start singing?

All the troubles that we face
Are lessons and experience
Deeper meaning mysterious
Be aware of what they're saying
Find the reason for your fear
When will you start dancing?

Gratitude is a great healer
Be thankful for the gift
It's meant to be a shift
To send you back to your true nature
Unconditional love alone
When will you start wondering?

By Anne Pollard

Quick Sand

Don't combat it they say,
For it will get worse
If you struggle and fight to survive.
But what happens the day
You succumb to the curse
Of this trap eating you alive.

For if you resist
Then death is quite certain
As your soul sinks quicker to despair.
But if only exist,
Death is even more certain,
Simply taking longer to get there.

And though you've tasted
How good life can be,
Somehow the thought only adds more pain.
Opportunity wasted,
You see the glass empty
Of the joys you were forced to abstain.

Do you lie there and hope?
Will someone throw you a line?
Do you pin your survival on others?
Do you reach out and grope?
Do you search for a sign?
Will your soul descend as it smothers?

Yet it hurts you so
To see those you've adored
Standing helpless, willing to try,
Because they all know
That their ropes are too short.
They can only watch as you slowly die.

So, which option is best?
Which one do you choose?
To die quickly or live on tormented?
Your mind needs a rest,
But either way you lose.
Either way, death can't be prevented.

By Jerry L Style

The Game

Let's play a game! he said
Sitting on a cloud
Oh! Sounds like fun, she said
As they all laughed out loud

What are the rules?
How do we play?
Rule number one:
Your free choice will stay

Rule number two:
(And here there's no slack)
What you send out
You always get back

We each get a costume
To wear and have fun
Whatever you want
Until the game is done

I'll be a rich man
I'll be a tree
I'll be a poor man
I'll be a mommy

OK! Sounds fun!
How do we start?
First, forget who you are
Then jump in your part

Oh! One final thing
Each night we stay
We meet at the cloud
And discuss our day

So they jumped in the spiral
Down to the game
Each on their path
None quite the same

The rich man had everything
His generosity great
He loved helping people
He loved to create

The tree grew tall
From the forest floor
He housed a bird's nest
And fed many more

The poor man had nothing
But his gratitude great
He learned to receive
And ignore all the hate

The mom had a child
That she tenderly loved
And as it grew up
She never judged

And every night
When the sun went down
They met at the cloud
And discussed what they found

They played the game
For a hundred years
Each had their joy
Each had their tears

And through the game
And along the way
They each remembered
It was just for play

When the game was done
They met at the cloud
And reviewed their lives
All beaming proud

What a fun game!
Let's do it again!
So they donned new costumes
And jumped back in

By Anne Pollard

Is this really you?

We all face decisions. We all have to choose.
Yes, many of my choices have gone the wrong way.
We all have our struggles. We all win or lose.
And loss makes you stronger and wiser they say.
But my heart has had all the wisdom it can take.
It's been broken too often before, it's true.
So, before I make another life changing mistake,
I just have to ask – Is this really you?

Are you really this caring? Are you really this sweet?
Are you this thoughtful and this empathetic?
On Halloween day, are you the trick or the treat?
Or is what's happening here again too prophetic?
Because if I've proven one thing – I've totally failed
At judging whether a person's character is true.
Will you be the same when your inner self is unveiled?
I just have to ask – Is this really you?

It's OK if what you've shown so far is incomplete.
No really. It's OK, I won't mind.
It's just when seeing different shades of deceit
It seems that I'm quite color blind.
So, if your heart is filled with revenge and loathing,
I beg you, please, just give me a clue.
Are you really a lamb, or a wolf in sheep's clothing?
Please tell me. Is this really you?

I suppose that I'm being very unfair to be
So blunt, asking such things from the start.
I guess you could ask the very same of me.
To seek out what's really in my heart.
Like I said at the beginning, we all have to choose,
And, I'm not asking to be wiser or for another life clue.
I'll believe what you say, even if I again lose.
So, this is me. Tell me, is this really you?

By Jerry L Style

The Root

It's been there for a hundred years
      This root upon the ground
Supporting a giant maple tree
      That stands so strong and proud

It meandered all across the path
      Winding like a snake
With bumps and humps along its spine
      A root, there's no mistake

As I walked along the path
      The grade began to rise
The root became a perfect step
      And thus, the perfect prize

So I sat down for a moment
      To admire its shape and length
Another Gaia miracle
      The embodiment of strength

A little squirrel came scampering through
      Looking for a place
To eat the acorn he had found
      The root, a perfect brace

I thought about the ancestors
　　　Who walked this path before
Was the root a help to them
　　　As they set out to explore

Then a robin flew my way
　　　A nut clutched in his beak
He needed something strong and hard
　　　To crack the nut to eat

It rained that day in the early morn
　　　And the root became the tool
For the water to puddle just a bit
　　　And form a tiny pool

A deer walked by and saw the place
　　　That offered her a drink
She slowly sipped the luscious wet
　　　The woods were so in sync

I wondered how deep that root had grown
　　　And then where it would end
But rose to move along the path
　　　Admiring my new friend

By Anne Pollard

Roots

A renowned poet once famously wrote
"I think that I shall never see
A poem as lovely as a tree…"
But at the risk of challenging that now famed quote.
I must respectfully disagree,
For the tree's real beauty lies hidden, for no one to see.

What the poet pointed out was the glamour, the glitz,
The proud, majestic, imposing and tall.
And he continued that it "… looks at God all day…"
But the tree he saw was like most hypocrites
For the "sacred" structure would definitely fall
With a strong wind that God will eventually send its way.

You see, what the poet said in his famous paradox
Was that the tree's real beauty truly lies,
Above ground in a spectacle for all to see.
But the tree's real beauty lies hidden, in mud and rocks
Spreading its roots to darkness, so not to compromise
The beauty above we now know as a tree.

Let me ask, where would the lovely tree be
Without the root supplied water or minerals or food?
Or the strength provided by its powerful earth grip?
And at the very start, the burgeoning seedling of the tree
Began by first spreading its roots, without gratitude,
Spreading its roots, taking second place in life's relationship.

So, remember, never, ever take for granted
The praise heaped upon you by those who only see
The obvious, the "lovely," the "true" attribute.
For those falsehoods will inevitably be recanted
For it's a fallacy that only God can create a tree.
No, "Only God can make a root."

By Jerry L Style

The Most Amazing Man

I met the most amazing man
Though only through a screen
His name was Kyle, "the angel guy"
And he opened doors unseen

He taught me love and angel guides
And gently reminded me
That we should share and never hide
The joy of eternity

He taught me how to close my eyes
And quietly go within
For it's in your heart and not the skies
Where the angels reign supreme

He taught me to have gratitude
And to ask them to come in
That's when I met Ezrael
My guardian angel and friend

He taught me to read angel cards
Which I now do every day
The amazing wisdom warms my heart
The messages come to stay

He taught me to read numbers
As a message from my guides
4:44 was the message tonight
100,000 angels with me abide

A Dance of Light and Dark

He taught me that the angels speak
Through animal spirits too
A tree, a rock and winding creek
Or a morning dove's sweet coo

He taught me how to meditate
And know that love is here
A moment where there is no hate
And there can be no fear

He taught me that we're all divine
And then to my surprise
The world became much more sublime
As I see it through angel eyes

With all my heart, I hope he knows
How many lives he's touched
For through his heart, energy flows
The world loves him so much

And then a miracle occurred
My teacher comes to town
I get to meet him face-to-face
My joy can know no bound!

Inspired by and written for Kyle Gray
By Anne Pollard

The Mirror of Your Soul

We all have our problems and unanswered prayers,
And things that we cannot control.
We all have our worries, issues and cares.
But what do we see in the mirror of our soul?

Is what the mirror shows a reflection of you?
Is the image you're seeing quite whole?
Are others to blame for what you're going through?
Or does the fault lie within your own soul?

I suppose it depends on who's doing the looking,
Or on whose eyes and mind are in control.
Because someone else might not see the same thing
When looking into the mirror of our very own soul.

Many find it so easy to point the finger of blame
At you, the person who they believe stole
Their reason for happiness, or their pain, their shame,
For the reason for the agony felt deep in their soul.

But their mirrors are faulty, warped and untrue.
And do not show the likenesses they should extol.
No, the vision they see isn't the real you,
Or the reflection of what's really deep in your soul.

But what I see in your mirror is one who truly cares.
Someone who's only trying to resolve and consol.
What I see in your mirror is someone who shares
The very same reflection, deep in my own soul.

By Jerry L Style

The Angel and the Indian

They walked beside little girl
The Angel and the Indian
    Angel on her right
    Indian on her left
An odd pair perhaps
Angelic realm and Indian past

The angel all in white
Wings to reach the sky
    He floated gently
    Glowed tremendously
But he was only a spirit
A 3rd eye fruition

The Indian in full regalia
Eagle feathers lined his staff
    A mighty sight
    If he could be seen
But he was only a spirit
A 3rd eye cognition

The woods called them all
Gaia in her most splendid form
    Spirits of the Earth
    Beckoned them on
A crooked tree pointed the way
A destination unknown

The Angel summoned the Archs
The mighty in their realm
    Michael, Gabriel
    Ariel, Jophiel
Each to bring their magic
Each to bring their spell

The Indian called the spirits
Emerging from behind every tree
      Whispers of suffering
      Whispers of love
Ethereal in presence
Riding on the wind

They came upon a traveler
But alas he could not see
      The Angel and
      The Indian
They were for the little girl
Her companions and her peace

They passed a gurgling brook
Where Gaia energy flowed
      Listen, said the Indian
      It will speak to you
Of ancient fountains
Of places yet to go

They stopped under a mighty tree
Branches split from lightening
      Reaching to angelic realms
      Wisdom of a thousand years
The Angel touched its bark
And blessed its fruitful leaves

The animals played among them
A squirrel of snowy white
      Sign of abundance
      Sign of ascension
The Indian bowed in reverence
The Angel smiled in delight

A Dance of Light and Dark

They had no need for words
Their thoughts alone enough
    Vibration strong
    Between the three
Connection of a higher source
Or roots beneath the trees

A symphony of sounds
So pleasing to the ear
    Birds of song
    Perfect harmony
Music touched the soul
There for all to hear

They came upon a fork
It was now time to depart
    Angel to the right
    Indian to the left
Little girl smiled and waved
Carrying both of them in her heart

By Anne Pollard

Waiting for the Rainbow

I've seen it myself,
So, I know that it's true!
A beautiful natural show.
That wondrous display
At the end of the storm
The spectacular, breathtaking rainbow.

And with all its natural beauty
It gives us a sign
That it's now safe to come and go.
And it gives us all hope
That there's better things to come –
A treasure at the end of the rainbow.

But in life, I have yet to see
Any signs of a parallel event,
There's no hint the storms will soon go.
No feeling of safety,
No beautiful displays.
No hope of experiencing life's rainbow.

Yet, I've lived through the storms,
Experienced the pain,
Suffered the hits blow by blow.
And I've listened to others
Who try to explain
That storms are necessary to form a rainbow.

But to protect my myself
From the constant storms,
I've locked my heart down far below.
Though protected from the tempest,
I cannot tell if it's over.
There's no chance of even seeing a rainbow.

So, do I keep my heart guarded
From risk of violent storm?
Can I survive another maddening woe?
Or do I allow it to go free,
Taking the risk once again
And stand unprotected, waiting for the rainbow?

by Jerry L Style

Earth Angel

You can't see my glorious wings
Unless you ask

You can't see my halo
Unless you look through your inner eyes

You can't hear my angel song
Unless you listen with your heart

I am an Earth Angel
I have the magic to heal
I have the strength of a thousand trees
I have the power to create worlds

I can see only good
In all creatures

I can see only love
For love is all there is

I can hear only music
Because music is your soul

I can't show you my full light
Because if I did, it would blind you

I can't sing in full voice
Because if I did, it would deafen you

But I can show you so much love
That it will inspire you to new heights

I am an Earth Angel

By Anne Pollard

When I'm With You

When I'm with you,
Held softly in your arms by you,
The pain all disappears from view,
When I'm with you.
There's no anguish and no sorrow,
There's no hurting and no fear about tomorrow.
That's when I'm with you,
Held softly in your arms.

When I'm with you,
Held softly in your arms by you,
Suddenly, the world is new,
When I'm with you.
And there's sunshine and there's flowers,
And there's laughter and there's ecstasy for hours.
That's when I'm with you,
Held softly in your arms.

The world seems full of fear and pain,
And it seems nobody cares,
But I can withstand almost anything
Just as long as you are there.

Because, when I'm with you,
Held softly in your arms by you,
We become one, we two,
When I'm with you.
And our passion flows a river.
Neither's a taker – each a lover and a giver.
That's when I'm with you,
Held softly in your arms.

When I'm with you,
Held softly in your arms by you,
Your love pierces me through and through.
When I'm with you.

By Jerry L Style

The Raptors

I do my hunting in the day
I can hear for miles away
Diving speed to catch my prey
My essence permeates the sky
Higher perspective from on high
My voice call, you can't deny

I AM THE HAWK

I do my hunting in the night
Completely silent when in flight
Rodents soothe my appetite
My ancient wisdom knows no bound
Mystic wonder so profound
A most distinctive call I sound

I AM THE OWL

My hunt starts when others' end
I soar and glide amidst the wind
Smelling miles around the bend
My patience is the rule of thumb
Bringing rebirth yet to come
I have no voice to speak from

I AM THE VULTURE

I am larger than the rest
Freedom and courage is my crest
My strength you should not test
I soar beyond the limitless sky
You know my familiar cry
Man, my enemy and ally

I AM THE EAGLE

By Anne Pollard

Next time... use a knife!

It was many years ago, now.
Was so early in our life.
When we took that holy, sacred vow,
And I took you for my wife.
But things have changed, and just don't know how.
Now there's sadness and there's hatred and there's anger and there's strife.
When you next feel the need to hurt me somehow,
Next time... use a knife!

I gave you all I've got to give.
I can't give you any more.
But your anger and your hatred live.
And can't walk out that door.
But the pain you give me hurts so deep
That I'm looking for the afterlife.
So beg you please, this promise keep.
Next time... use a knife!

Many years I've tried to do what's right.
Many years I've sacrificed.
But it's no good for you, and I feel your spite.
And with my heart I've paid the price.
But the pain I feel stays out of sight
And it boils and it festers and contaminates my life.
So let the pain flow freely here tonight.
Next time... use a knife!

If you use a knife, it'll soon be done,
With my blood flowing on the floor.
In your battle of words, you'll know you've won,
And I'll know I'll feel pain no more.
And you'll finally see the pain you brought,
In red puddles of my life.
So remember please, this one small thought.
Next time... use a knife!

A Dance of Light and Dark

All my life I've loved you for what you are;
All the good things and the bad.
But your fears have changed just who you are,
And it's ruined what we've had.
Now you can't love me or who I am.
And your hatred flows like water, and it's drowning out my life.
So, end it all, just end it! Damn!
Next time... use a knife!

I've given you all I've got to give.
I can't give you any more.
But your anger and your hatred live.
And I can't walk out that door.
But the pain you give me hurts so deep
That I'm looking for the afterlife.
So beg you please, this promise keep.
Next time... use a knife!

By Jerry L Style

The Shaman

He quietly walks through the woods
    Barefoot if he can
To commune with all of nature
    Offering in hand

It is sacred tobacco
    That he carries in his pack
To offer to the perfect tree
    To relieve his aching back

He was dancing with some friends, you see
    To relieve some training stress
And went a little overboard
    Now his back was in distress

He found the tree that called to him
    And asked if it would mend
When "yes" the answer given
    The offering would transcend

He sat down with the tree
    Put his back against the trunk
Then sent prayers of thankfulness
    And to his heart he sunk

The cure was not immediate
    But in the day to come
The backache was a distant thought
    The healing work was done

The Shaman also works with guides
    The animal spirit kind
He understands their gift to us
    And how we are intwined

A Dance of Light and Dark

He can take you on a journey
    Down into Mother Earth
And reveal your power animal
    The one you had at birth

He speaks to the ancestors
    And honors their domain
That helps us heal our past
    And ease ancestral pain

He learned the sacred ceremonies
    Of those that came before
He scribed them for posterity
    Hoping others would explore

But the most important thing he does
    Is mentor eager folk
Because he knows, to heal the world
    Love should be invoked

He shares his wisdom freely
    As all good Shaman do
And rejoices in the time
    When his graduate breaks through

So how, you ask, do I know
    This Universal charmer
Well, he is *my* mentor
    Dr. Steven Farmer

By Anne Pollard

The Release Ceremony

i go to find, with penitent heart
my choice to release is scribed
the sacred release ceremony now to start
"i choose to release" prescribed

along the wooded trail i seek
the effigy to see
a rock, a stick, or simple leaf
i feel it drawn to me

i find a stone, shroud in mist
and gently hold it close
i ask its willingness to assist
am answered "yes, of course"

returning home with rock in hand
i envelop it with paper
that holds the words of my intention
then leave it on the table

as i drift to peaceful sleep
i thank my spirit guides
for moving my intention deep
to the rock it now abides

i dream of love and sweet release
the image bold and clear
my soul is moving toward its peace
an angel choir i hear

release day comes, to the woods i go
now to find a tree
one with such an aura glow
it naturally speaks to me

A Dance of Light and Dark

the mighty oak, so tall and strong
of course, the perfect choice
i don't have to wander long
i hear its inner voice

i kneel before the mighty oak
and say a prayer of thanks
then dig a hole to hold the oath
and set the prayer aflame

the smoke goes up to father sky
the prayer to mother earth
the release is done before my eyes
the release to the universe

another sacred prayer of thanks
as a lone hawk calls above
the ceremony, full of grace
walking back to love

now i wait to see the end
of the sacred release rite
i know my soul is free to send
the pain to brilliant light

for my intention is manifest
i feel that in my heart
the harmony is at its best
the end is now the start

Inspired by the Release Ceremony from Dr. Steven Farmer

By Anne Pollard

Smoldering Greeting Card Ashes

I can still see you patiently standing there
In the pharmacy's greeting card aisle
As you picked out each greeting card with great care
Each one with its own special message and style.
Every card required a tempo, a beat.
More than just words were important to you.
And if the card wasn't quite right or somehow incomplete
You added your own thoughts to make it ring true.

And it didn't matter who the recipient was,
Your daughter, your grandson, your friend.
You kept looking for the perfect card because
Each one had to show how you felt 'til the end.
As your lover and spouse, I received many from you, too –
Each one – a carefully heartfelt selection.
Whether a birthday, a Valentine, anniversary, or just from you
Expressing how much you loved our never-ending connection.

I diligently saved each and every cherished card
For the words and their meaning touched my heart.
They were so precious to me that I could never discard
Your loving cards which said we'd never part.

\/

A Dance of Light and Dark

But now you've abandoned, and all those cards I've received
Now confess that you were lying all the while.
Each card now saying I should have never believed
Lay there on the floor in a crumpled-up pile.

Does "always" mean "always", or to you, does it end?
Does "eternal" have some unknown connotation?
When you said that you'd marry me again and again,
Was it just a meaningless conversation?
When your cards said you loved the life we built together,
And how you loved the special way that I was treating,
Was there a clue that you changed the meaning of "forever,"
Or that your cards should have never been deemed "greeting?"

So, as I now sit and light the crumpled card-pile on fire,
It occurs to me that I'm not the only one who
Was so wrongfully deceived – do others know you're a liar?
Would they throw their crumple cards into the blazing fire, too?
And I am awed at the ease the flaming greeting cards stoke
Spontaneous combustion caused when promise and truth clashes.
And how quickly your carefully chosen lies go up in smoke –
Rising up from the smoldering greeting card ashes.

By Jerry L Style

Did You Know You Had a Choice?

In the hospital on your death bed
Did you know you have a choice?
Suffering and scared of what's ahead
Did you know you have a choice?
Looking at the end with fear and dread
Did you know you have a choice?

Even in the last hours
Your soul is ready to soar
It's a new beginning, not an ending
It's back to your infinite core
You get to review your really cool life
No one is judging you anymore
Only love and beauty everywhere
And infinity to explore

And time dissolves
And space dissolves
And ego disappears

Get ready for the next adventure!
Back to earth school to play
Or off to a distant galaxy
Choose your next ballet
A body or a light being
So many options to survey
Infinite time
New adventure on the way

So you choose your exit path
Did you know you have a choice?

By Anne Pollard

We're already there

Author's Note:
This poem is so filled with self-loathing, self-pity and anger that
I've been ashamed to admit that I authored it
and have hesitated to include it among these works.
But I realized that you, the reader just might feel the same way
that I expressed in this poem during those dark days of my life.
If you have those same feelings, you have my deepest sympathies.
And, while I cannot tell you that things happen for a reason,
I can say that bad things indeed do happen
and that life is about how we deal with those things.
I, myself have made it through those dark days. You will, too.

"Everything happens for a reason," they say.
"It's all part of God's grand design."
"Just ignore the pain, it'll all go away,"
"Stop complaining. It will turn out to be just fine."
"God really does love you," they fervently claim.
"He'd never let bad things happen to you!"
"So just suck it up, there's no one to blame."
"You'll understand it all when your life is through."

"Don't ask why villains fly fully loaded planes
Into buildings, killing thousands of innocents."
"Don't ask why violent hurricanes
Destroy those without any means of defense."
"Don't question why your heart's been broken
More times than you'd care to admit."
Questions of 'Why?' must endlessly be unspoken.
Just shut up and put up with all of the shit.

Yet life must go on, but there's so much of life remaining.
A thought not particularly reassuring.
And the "they" who tell you to stop your complaining
Don't understand that life-long pains remain enduring.
But they still promise that God will make it all turn out well,
That there's a reason for this ongoing nightmare.
So, you fight off the urges to tell "them" to all go to hell,
Because sadly, you realize that we're already there.

by Jerry L Style

The Empty House

The little house was deathly still
Barely any furniture remained
Almost like an empty shell
After sixty years sustained

I came to check, like I always do
To make sure things looked good
The empty house was now for sale
In the old neighborhood

I finished chores and was set to leave
When I had a sudden feeling
Maybe I should sit a spell
And do a little healing

I went into the living room
And found my favorite chair
I sat down and took a breath
Then said a little prayer

Recalling all the memories
Of a family life gone by
And as I sat there by myself
I had a little cry

Not for sadness or regret
Not for past mistakes
But for the sweetest memories
That a loving parent makes

I longed to feel their touch again
A bittersweet embrace
To laugh at daddy's silly grin
To see my mama's face

But they both died some time ago
Souls released once more
Into the All That Is
For new worlds to explore

So I just sat and closed my eyes
To feel the energy here
And humbly called upon my guides
To draw their presence near

I hear a bump, could that be them?
I stop my breathing to listen again
And then I laugh and realize
It's just the fridge kicking in

So I take a breath and feel my heart
Looking for a thought to hold
I conjure up their wedding rings
And it all started to unfold

The vision of the funeral
When daddy passed away
Mom searching for her wedding ring
Ending in dismay

We couldn't find it anywhere
It was such a teaser
Then months later, laughing
When she found it in the freezer

I smiled, remembering the happiness
Of that crazy, funny day
And I think it drew them closer
My connection was underway

I began to feel a presence
Permeate the space
There were two separate energies
I knew I must embrace

There was no sound, there was no scene
Just feelings to absorb
An energy presence of these beings
And love poured from these orbs

A Dance of Light and Dark

They held me in a crucible
And made sure that I knew
I was loved beyond measure
And would always hold these two

And then another presence came
The angels from the sky
A thousand-fold were with me
I could only sit and cry

I stayed there for a while
And hoped it would not end
Such an incredible feeling
So hard to comprehend

But the energy finally faded
And I opened up my eyes
To see an empty house again
I had said my goodbyes

I don't yet know who it will be
Who makes this house their home
But I know that love will hold them
As they enter their new throne

Only few will get this poem
And that's OK by me
You see, it's just *my* journey
But I share for all to see

So others may understand
A connection that is real
And maybe not one you see
But one you only feel

To open these connections
Your heart space is the key
And then you can feel a loved one
Somewhere you won't foresee

By Anne Pollard

Goose Pond

It's not a place where all belong,
Though its warmth bids those who go there –
Come! Unite with nature's precious song –
Encounter beauty everywhere!
Cherish the serenity, secluded, sincere.
Here, God has waved his magic wand.
Escape life's folly, anxiety and fear,
At this wonderful place called Goose Pond.

Stand beneath night skies on a frozen lake.
Count the uncountable stars overhead.
Witness the creation of a new daybreak;
Mountain tops ablaze in the sun's orangy-red.
Barron trees coat snow covered hills like hair,
But there's no reason to fear or abscond,
Though seemingly beset by a huge hibernating bear
At this enchanted place called Goose Pond.

Listen to the silence as it speaks to your soul.
Hear its meaning and how it is spoken.
Carefully answer and never lose self-control,
For the silence is so easily broken.
Yet amaze at the distance a voice can be heard,
And how the mountains politely respond;
Repeating your message word-for-word,
At this spiritual place called Goose Pond.

Don't worry of the smallness of yourself.
Don't let the sheer vastness overwhelm.
For here, you're vital as everything else.
Here, you're under God's realm.
People of love will soon gather near,
Whether in this life or beyond,
To share with each other without anger or fear
At a heavenly place like Goose Pond.

By Jerry L Style

Autumn Leaves

It's all so very peaceful
To stand among the trees
Autumn makes its final show
Look at the colors in the leaves

Yellow, orange, and bright red too
The colors are astounding
So many leaves upon the ground
But many more abounding

I love the changing seasons
Soon the trees are off to sleep
Except for the evergreens
Who have their color to keep

Now you can see the nests
That were built up in the sky
Oh, so warm and comfortable
As an autumn breeze blows by

Some trees are already bare
And dropped their final leaf
Now ready for winter slumber
They've fallen off to sleep

But most of the leaves are hanging on
Brilliant to the last
For giving up those leaves
Is such a final task

The leaves are thick as pudding
And already to my knees
It's fun to walk amongst them
Even though it makes me sneeze

The mailman comes around the bend
WAIT! Where has my mind been?
Oh, standing in my own front yard
I better rake again!

By Anne Pollard

A N N E   P O L L A R D   A N D   J E R R Y   L   S T Y L E

Hit a home run, Mick!

The little boy was playing hard, scraping up his knee,
Tears streaming down his reddened cheeks, he ran in from the April sun.
Mom took him in, dried his eyes, she knew just how to be.
She gave the little one a kiss, then turned the tv on.
The game was on, the Yanks were down, the score was 4 to 3.
But #7 was up, young phenomenon, and the boy shouted out a plea –
"Hit a home run, Mick! Hit a home run! Hit a home run for me!"

His eyes were fixed on the tv screen, the crowd began to roar.
The little one sat there breathless, hoping, adoring his paragon.
The Mick took a mighty swing and the ball began to soar;
It was deep, deep, deep to left – going, going, gone!
The crowd went wild, Mick started his trot and the tyke danced around in glee.
The pain in his battered knee had gone and he yelled out a symphony!
"You hit a home run, Mick! You hit a home run! You hit a home run for me!"

The quiet teen always did his best, but rarely was it good enough.
He competed at sports, at grade, at girls, but failed by comparison.
But Dad would say, "Let's have a catch," but when things got a little too rough,
The boy knew frustration would end real soon when he turned the television on.
In July's blazing heat, veteran Mick at the plate, it was easy to foresee
That his troubles all would be forgotten, it was a matter of destiny:
"Hit a home run, Mick! Hit a home run! Hit a home run for me!"

The young married man had the world on his back, young wife and family.
He sacrificed all to make ends meet; running life's marathon,
His wife's too busy and didn't understand why sometimes he would flee
From life's constant worries and demands and then turn the Yankees on.
The aging Mick could barely walk, but strove on in his agony.
And under fall skies, he'd often strike out, but he'd bring back the memory:
"Hit a home run, Mick! Hit a home run! Hit a home run for me!"

A Dance of Light and Dark

The middle-aged man was not doing well, confused by life's irony
And no matter how hard a person worked, the effort would be undone.
His happiness absent, contentment was gone, truly life's refugee.
And he sat there and thought of his life in review, and tried to remember the fun.
But Mom's kiss didn't help and Dad was dead, and his wife acted scornfully.
In December's short days, Mick, too, was gone, and there's no one to answer his plea –
"Hit a home run, Mick! Hit a home run! Hit a home run for me!"

"My Mick! My Mick!" he cried in the dark, "Why have you forsaken me?!
How could you retire and leave me like this? I'll get you for this, Mick – I swear!
You were my life's anesthesia, Mick, for only you could guarantee
That the pain in my life would end for a while – to that no one else could compare!
So please Mick, come back and save me! Help end this catastrophe!"
But there in the dark, no one answered his prayer, so he shouted defiantly –
"Hit a home run, Mick! Hit a home run! Hit a home run for me!"

The little boy was playing hard, scraping up his knee.
So, Grandpa held him and gave him a kiss, consoling the little one.
Then he entranced the child with tales of his youth, about Mick and the pain he'd free.
But he warned, "Find happiness inside yourself, and not from what others have done,"
But as winter's death turned to spring's new life, though the boy listened innocently,
The old man's advice fell on ears too young, for the tyke yelled instinctively –
"Hit a home run, Mick! Hit a home run! Hit a home run for me!"

By Jerry L Style

Hairy Trees

I was walking through Savannah
And saw the strangest thing
All the trees had hair!
It was kinda like their bling

Some was long and scraggily
Some was short and trim
But no matter what the shape
It hung from every limb

There were lots of shades of grey
And it seemed to weave together
Clearly, by the amount there was
It could survive most any weather

It was really quite unusual
As it swayed among the breeze
What on earth is this hair?
Could it be a disease?

I wondered how on earth it grew
It didn't have a root
It must be something magical
My interest was acute!

I reached up to touch it
This crazy looking hair
It wasn't soft or silky
I had nothing to compare

I was more confused than ever
But then began to see
The beauty that it brought
To each and every tree

So I asked my friend what it was
Because I was at a loss
She said "Silly girl,
That's just Spanish Moss"

By Anne Pollard

110

HOMELESS

HE SAT THERE, ALONE, IN HIS CARDBOARD SHACK;
HIS CLOTHES FULL OF HOLES, HIS FACE WORN AND GRAY.
THIS NAMELESS, DECREPIT, LONELY, BOTHERSOME MAN IN BLACK
HAD FORGOTTEN HOW TO SMILE, TO LAUGH, FORGOTTEN HOW TO PRAY.
AND HE WONDERED, "HOW'D I GET HERE? WHAT WAS IT MY LIFE LACKED?"
"WHAT CAUSED MY LIFE SUCH AGONY, AND CAUSED MY PATH TO STRAY?"
"I THOUGHT I ALWAYS DID MY VERY BEST. SO WHY AM I SO ATTACKED?"
"WHAT COULD I HAVE DONE DIFFERENTLY? WHAT TOOK MY LIFE AWAY?"
AFTER MUCH SOUL SEARCHING HE FINALLY REALIZED THE SAD FACT
THAT HE'D GIVEN ONLY TO THE TAKERS. AND MUCH TO HIS DISMAY,
THAT TAKERS JUST KEEP TAKING, LEAVING HIM TOTALLY RACKED.
AND THE GIVERS HE'D KNOWN WERE USED UP, LEFT TO DECAY,
BY THE TAKERS, DRAINING THEM TOO, RAPING TO BE EXACT.
HE JUST HAD NO MORE LEFT TO GIVE; LIFE'S IN DISARRAY,
HE FINALLY UNDERSTOOD – HE WAS NOT GIVEN BACK
THE LOVE HE SO NEEDED TO HELP HIS PAIN ALLAY.
AND IT'S TRUE THAT ALL THE GIVERS ATTRACT
ALL THE MANY TAKERS EAGER TO BETRAY.
FOR, THOSE WHO TAKE WILL TAKE –
AND THOSE VERY FEW GIVERS –
GIVE THEIR LIFE AWAY.
DAMN!

By Jerry L Style

On The Beach

The sun on my face
The warmth on my skin
Archangel Uriel
Is at it again

My little beach towel
Is just a nit
On a vast sandy beach
With no limit

The sun so intense
I lose my will
To move or think
I just want to be still

The sound of the ocean
A few feet away
The rumble of people
At rest and at play

As I soak in the light
And lie perfectly still
I am in utter bliss
I can't get my fill

The sand supports
My body contour
Heaven on earth
For me that's assured

There is no past
No yet to come
Just perfect now
And I succumb

My mind drifts
To a galaxy far away
Do they have beaches
With such sun display

I hope they do
It's beyond the best
To love the sun
And love the rest

So I lay here basking
In the glorious sun
Words can't describe
The infinite union

My joy is immense
In this fabulous scene
But as Hippo Spirit says
Don't forget to wear sunscreen!

By Anne Pollard

WHY TRY?

BECAUSE WHEN WE TRY
WE GIVE OFF LITTLE RAYS OF LIGHT.
IT DOESN'T MATTER WHETHER WE SUCCEED OR NOT.
IT'S ONLY IN TRYING THAT WE SHINE.
THESE RAYS OF LIGHT WE GIVE OFF
TRAVEL FROM PERSON TO PERSON.
MOST PEOPLE JUST ABSORB THE LIGHT,
KEEPING IT ALL FOR THEMSELVES…
IT MAKES IT TOUGH TO TRY.

BUT, WITHOUT EVEN KNOWING IT,
SOME OF THE LIGHT WE GIVE OFF IS TAKEN IN BY A FEW
AND THEN SENT OUT AGAIN.
OR, EVEN BETTER YET,
SOME OF THE LIGHT WARMS THE ABSORBERS SO MUCH
THAT THEY NOW GIVE OFF LIGHT, TOO.

THAT'S WHAT HAPPENED WITH YOU.
YOU WEREN'T BORN GIVING OFF LIGHT.
SOMEONE SHINED ON YOU.
NOW YOU SHINE ON OTHERS.

AND A FUNNY THING ABOUT THOSE
WHO ONLY ABSORB THE LIGHT…
UNLESS A PERSON REFLECTS LIGHT,
THEY SIMPLY DISAPPEAR.

SO, DON'T STOP TRYING.
THE WORLD WOULD BE
A MUCH DARKER PLACE.

By Jerry L Style

Insomnia

It's 3 AM and I'm up again
My soul journey tonight has come to an end
I roll over and hope it's a passing thing
And sleep will resume if I can just allow it in

It's 3:05 and sleep remains illusive
So I get out of bed and go downstairs
A glass of water perhaps to soothe my thirst
The sweet nectar of life, cold and wet

It's 3:10 and I try the fire
The only sound is the puff of the gas as it lights the logs
There's a chill in the house and the heat feels good
I stare at the blue flames that sear my scratchy eyes

It's 3:15 and I think about yesterday
It was a wonderful day, full of joy
The walk in the woods, so quiet and peaceful
Where is that peace now?

It's 3:20 and I hope it's done
Chasing the sleep that still won't come
I go back upstairs and crawl into bed
The sheets are cold and it feels good on my skin

It's 3:25 and I close my eyes
There is a full moon tonight and the light seeps through the blinds
I should have drawn the curtains
Maybe the darkness would have enveloped my mind

It's 3:30 and my legs start to twitch
The final blow for any hope of more sleep
So I get up again and go downstairs
There's an owl softly hooting to me in the backyard

It's 3:35 and I sit on the floor
I stretch my legs to help with the restlessness
It feels good to find the perfect pose
That touches the muscles just right

It's 3:40 and I decide to try the couch
The firmness against my back feels nice
I pull up the blanket that drapes my new bed
I close my eyes and breathe, hoping sleep returns

It's 3:45 and I can feel the world sleeping without me
The stretching helped, but not enough
My legs are twitching again, restless once more
So I throw off the blanket and get up again

It's 3:50 and I hear the rain start to fall
Maybe that rhythmic beat will lull me to sleep
But my mind is too busy now, I've been up too long
I know the trying will now be in vain

It's 3:55 and I go back upstairs
Not to bed this time, but to get dressed
The writing muse has now awoken as well
So I'll take advantage of the quiet and create

It's 4:00 and I have pen to paper
Doesn't matter really, I have no place to be
So I put on the coffee and enjoy my muse
Insomnia can also set you free

By Anne Pollard

The Picture

Trapped up here upon the shelf, imprisoned by the glass,
Entombed in exile of the self, waiting for days to pass.

Looking out in search of life, the crystal seems so clear.
Answer to the trials and strife seems so painfully near.

But the glass prevents the reaching out of arms yearning to hold tight.
And it causes anger, causes doubt, causes questions, wrong or right.

If existence up here can cause such pain, why is it so prolonged?
But what right is there to complain when allowing self to be wronged?

Yet, to break the glass would cut and maim those close, tearing them apart.
And even I would never be the same with the shredding of my heart.

But how long can I resist attacks? Will the pain felt redefine me?
Will I be marred by lines and cracks? Who will emerge when finally free?

So, here I stay, enduring all the harms – complete denial of the self.
Waiting to be held in someone's arms, but I'm trapped up here on the shelf.

By Jerry L Style

Finding Joy

May you find your biggest joys in the smallest pleasures…

The little bird who flew by your window
The song that had the great crescendo

The TV show that made you laugh
Or soaking in a bubble bath

Your new grandchild with big bright eyes
Millions of stars in the night skies

The strawberry that you picked to eat
The trusted friend you have plans to meet

The cute little poem that made you smile
The satisfaction of the final mile

A crooked tree with a funny face
The gentle gift of a warm embrace

A babbling brook meandering on
The sweet taste left in your mouth when the chocolate is gone

A warm cozy bed as you fall asleep
These are the joys I wish you to keep

By Anne Pollard

About the Authors

Anne Pollard is an award-winning author from Charlotte, NC. She had a long, successful career in Information Technology as a Senior Director and CIO for various companies.

During her role as a senior leader, she mentored and inspired numerous colleagues in both business and personal goal achievement.
She is now retired from the corporate life and enjoys writing, gardening, traveling, riding motorcycles and spending time with her family and friends.

She is passionate about living your best life, whatever that is for you, and being grateful for the infinite abundance we all have.
Find out about her other books at www.Anne-Pollard.com!

Jerry Style is not who you would consider to be your typical author or poet. He has had a long and successful career as a tax and financial planner for thousands of clients, attributing his success not to his tax/financial knowledge, but to his ability to relate to his clients, regardless of their financial well-being.

As is true of many, Jerry has gone through lengthy periods of agonizing emotional pain. As he describes it, he was "saved" by a poet that occupied his mind and body, typically "visiting" him during the wee hours of the morning. This invading poet allowed Jerry to not only put a voice to his pain in a way that many can relate, but to search for and find the answers we all seek.

Jerry is now retired, and is focused on getting through the pain and to putting an end to always being the victim. Jerry feels that it is through his connection with Anne Pollard, he is now beginning to understand that experiencing loss intrinsically means that you had something to lose to begin with. Therefore, don't grieve what you've lost. Instead, celebrate what you've had and can have again.